The Plant Love Kitchen

The Plant Love Kitchen

AN EASY GUIDE TO PLANT-FORWARD EATING, WITH 75+ RECIPES

Marisa Moore

R.D.N., L.D.

NATIONAL GEOGRAPHIC

WASHINGTON, D.C.

Contents

Introduction

Thank you for picking up *The Plant Love Kitchen* and trusting me to guide you on this journey to add more plants to your plate. I hope this book will motivate you to explore a few new plant foods and relieve any pressure you've felt to go fully vegan or vegetarian. This journey is all about what is the best fit for you, and throughout I offer flexible approaches and dishes that allow you to try new foods without forsaking old favorites. Cheers to trying new things and to a shift toward eating more plants—one bite at a time!

MY JOURNEY TO PLANT-FORWARD EATING

I grew up in the Carolinas, in the rural southern United States. I was raised on okra and tomatoes, fish and grits, field peas and collard greens, corn bread and lots of rice. Neck bones, chicken, and fatback were on the table regularly—but so were farm-fresh butter beans, cabbage, sweet corn, peaches, and blueberries. When I was old enough to drive and became busy with high school, I also had my share of boxed mac and cheese, personal pan pizzas, and fast-food burgers and fries.

But I never *really* liked meat. I was always more interested in everything else on the plate. I was the kid at the table trying to pick the meat out of the spaghetti and meat sauce. When I went to college, I quickly started learning about and experimenting with being vegan. I didn't know what tofu was before this. At the time, plant milk (soy or rice milk in a shelf-stable box) was relegated to a dusty corner in the back of the supermarket. Kale was still just a garnish on the plate.

I was vegan or vegetarian throughout college, much to the curiosity of my friends and family. But they went with it, making the green beans without meat just for me during the holidays. Eventually, I added a few things back to my diet, mostly chicken and fish. I have enjoyed the flexibility.

Fast-forward many years later, and I am clear. While I prefer plants, I eat other foods when I want. I don't need to stick to a vegan or vegetarian label. With an eye toward preventing chronic disease and feeling my best, I eat what my body needs at the time.

And I've shared my philosophy with clients over the years in my work as a registered dietitian nutritionist. From one-on-one sessions focused on managing blood pressure or blood glucose levels to group cooking classes to in-depth conversations with the media, I delight in helping people find their own balance when it comes to eating and overall wellness.

WHAT'S TO LOVE ABOUT PLANT LOVE?

Throughout these pages you'll find tips and tricks to help you achieve a plant-forward plate with flexibility in mind. Here is what you can expect:

- Well-researched information on the benefits of a plant-forward way of eating
- Tips to help you set yourself up for success
- Guides and cheat sheets to quickly reference when cooking grains, beans, and vegetables
- More than 75 flexible recipes to help you kick off your journey to plant-forward eating
- *The Plant Love Kitchen* meal plans that meet you where you are
- "Love Notes" with nutritional facts about the food you're eating

THANK YOU FOR BEING HERE

The Plant Love Kitchen is for anyone who wants to add more plants to the plate. Research suggests that while many people aren't willing to go completely vegan or vegetarian, they are willing and ready to reduce the amount of meat they eat. That's where my plant-forward approach finds the happy medium. I'm excited to help you start the journey!

Note: The recipes in *The Plant Love Kitchen* were developed with flexibility in mind. You'll see that the majority of the recipes that contain animal products also have a plant-based alternative for a vegan or vegetarian option. For example, my Make-Ahead Spinach Breakfast Wraps (page 83) can be made with whole eggs or a plant-based liquid egg substitute in the same amount. My Sheet Pan Fajitas recipe (page 178) has instructions for both a fish and a portobello mushroom option.

Select images are from my Instagram (@marisamoore) or feature recipes available on my blog, marisamoore.com.

A Plant-Powered Life

Part 1

Plant-Forward Eating and Your Health

WHAT IS PLANT-FORWARD?

PLANT-FORWARD PUTS PLANTS FIRST.

By that I mean, plant-forward eating centers plant-based foods. It emphasizes fruits, vegetables, legumes, grains, nuts, and seeds as the star of the plate but doesn't limit what you eat to plant-based foods only. It's a way of cooking and eating, but most important, it's a shift in mindset.

PLANT-FORWARD IS NOT ALL-OR-NOTHING

While plants are the star, this approach allows you to also enjoy eggs, dairy, and meat anytime you want, if you want. The big difference: Animal-based foods are not the main focus on your plate, as they are in the standard American diet.

Now, you might be wondering how plant-forward differs from plant-based, vegetarian, or vegan ways of eating. There are some big differences. Let's get into it.

PLANT-FORWARD As part of their Menus of Change program, the Culinary Institute of America and the Harvard T. H. Chan School of Public Health's Department of Nutrition define "plant-forward" as "a style of cooking and eating that emphasizes and celebrates, but is not limited to, plant-based foods—including fruits and vegetables (produce); whole grains; beans, other legumes (pulses), and soy foods; nuts and seeds; plant oils; and herbs and spices—and that reflects evidence-based principles of health and sustainability."

While it's sort of an umbrella term that can include vegan, vegetarian, flexitarian, and other eating habits, I like to think of plant-forward as less a diet and more a way of thinking. It shines a light on plants and allows you to put them first. Plant-forward is a mindset shift that puts plants at the center of the plate, versus off to the side; it also doesn't require you to completely give up anything else.

Plant-forward eating encourages creativity and is accessible to anyone. I've seen it in practice, and recent survey data reveals that nearly one in four Americans has recently cut back on how much meat they eat. Health is cited as the overwhelming reason for cutting back on meat, but many are also concerned about the environment, animal welfare, and food safety. Maybe you can relate?

FLEXITARIAN VS. PLANT-FORWARD Plant-forward is very similar to flexitarian eating (in which a person might be mostly vegetarian but occasionally eats meat or fish), and many might say they are the same. However, the term "plant-forward" helps really put the focus on plants. And remember that "plant-forward" refers to the style of cooking and the overall mindset of the way you eat.

PLANT-BASED While "plant-forward" focuses on a style of cooking and a way of eating, the term "plant-based" refers to the food itself—the ingredients. That's the vegetables, fruits, grains, nuts, and legumes used in a plant-forward way of eating. Though there is no official definition, "plant-based" often means vegan, but not always. So if you're ever not sure, ask.

VEGETARIAN A vegetarian diet does not include meat, seafood, or poultry but may include milk, cheese, and eggs. You may hear the term "lacto-vegetarian," which means that a person's diet includes dairy foods. Lacto-ovo-vegetarians eat both eggs and dairy foods. Lacto-ovo-vegetarians enjoy the most flexibility and have fewer nutrition gaps to close. Much of the research cited in this book is based on vegetarian diets. And if you're curious, according to a 2018 Gallup poll, 5 percent of Americans identify as vegetarian.

VEGAN A vegan diet excludes all animal-based foods, including dairy and those made by animals, such as honey and additives, food dyes, and binders made with or by insects. This way of eating is 100 percent plant-based, with abundant fruits, vegetables, grains, legumes, and nuts, and does require a bit of extra attention and planning to make sure you get adequate and balanced nutrition. But that can be said for any diet.

SHOULD YOU GO PLANT-FORWARD?

That's totally up to you!

A plant-forward approach can fit into any lifestyle or culture and can be appropriate no matter your health practices and goals. In fact, plant-forward eating isn't new.

Many traditional diets such as the African Heritage and Mediterranean—both of which have been well researched—already make plants the star of the plate.

As much as we talk about eating more fruits and vegetables, most adults don't get enough. Data from the Centers for Disease Control and Prevention reveals that nine out of 10 American adults don't get the recommended amount of fruits and vegetables per day. If you're in that number (or not), I'm hoping this book will help you get more than enough fruits and vegetables each day—with ease.

Plant-forward works for those who are comfortable without labels. It leaves the door open to enjoy traditional foods on holidays or while on vacation without the worries or guilt associated with straying from a specific diet. It's an inclusive way of eating that is flexible, nourishing, and packed with flavor and good-for-you ingredients. Plus, there are lots of potential health benefits.

PLANT-FORWARD BENEFITS

Research continues to mount in support of eating more plants to help reduce the risk of chronic diseases, such as heart disease, diabetes, and some cancers, while improving overall health, wellness, and longevity.

Thanks to the diversity of nutrients plants provide, a plant-forward approach offers a variety of potential health and nutrition benefits:

LOWERED RISK FOR METABOLIC SYNDROME Vegan diets specifically are associated with a reduced risk of metabolic syndrome, a precursor condition to heart disease, type 2 diabetes, and stroke.

SUPPORT FOR HEART HEALTH Research suggests that diets high in plant foods and low in animal foods are associated with a lower risk for developing cardiovascular disease, and they decrease the risk of dying from heart disease and other causes.

LONGER LIFE EXPECTANCY Eating the recommended amounts of fruits and vegetables is associated with a lower risk of death from cardiovascular disease in particular, but also from cancer and other causes. There's also evidence that a higher consumption of plant protein (compared with animal sources) is associated with living longer overall.

BETTER GUT HEALTH If you've ever tried a vegan or vegetarian diet after eating lots of fast-food burgers, you may have immediately noticed a difference in how your body feels. Maybe you noticed better regularity and felt like your digestive system got an upgrade overnight. Plants drive those changes with lots of fiber and other gut-friendly components!

Plant-based diets are good for the gut. And what's good for the gut is good for immune health and a number of other health effects, including mental health.

REDUCED RISK FOR CERTAIN CANCERS Research links a diet with lots of plants to lower rates of certain cancers. Researchers believe that plants offer some protection, thanks to being rich sources of a variety of bioactive plant compounds that help protect our cells from damage. This is an area that needs more research, but we know that plants are rich in cancer-fighting components, including fiber and abundant vitamins, minerals, and phytonutrients with antioxidant properties.

WEIGHT MANAGEMENT It may be easier to manage your weight on a plant-based diet. With a focus on plants, you're bound to get more fiber, which is filling and satisfying.

GOOD FOR THE PLANET Choosing plant-based foods more often and cutting back on the amount of meat you eat is generally better for the environment. This is because, in the grand scheme of things, producing plants for food is more sustainable than producing animals for food. Plants generally require fewer natural resources and produce fewer greenhouse gas emissions and waste products.

In reviewing these benefits, do keep in mind that much of the research may have been done with people who have easy access to fruits and vegetables. Whether a person has access to fruits and vegetables and other socioeconomic factors can play a major role in health outcomes.

GETTING THE NUTRIENTS YOU NEED

How are you going to get your protein? I was asked this question over and over again when I was vegan. And it's the same question I get now as a registered dietitian nutritionist anytime a client (or random person at a party) decides to cut out meat or eat less of it. But the really good news is that you can easily obtain adequate and quality protein from plants!

With meat at the center of the standard American diet, it's natural to wonder whether eating less meat will result in nutrient deficiencies. Thankfully, the plant-forward approach eliminates a lot of the common concerns associated with following a vegan diet.

But if you are making a significant shift, here are a few nutrients to keep in mind as you transition from a diet that's high in animal foods to one with less.

PROTEIN Contrary to popular belief, getting protein from plants is not hard. It's actually pretty easy with just a little forethought. Common plant protein options include edamame (young soybeans), tofu, tempeh, beans, peas, lentils, nuts, and seeds. But when using a plant-forward approach, you also have the option to eat eggs and other animal protein too.

To get adequate amino acids (the molecules that combine to make proteins, which are the building blocks of the body), choose a variety of plant protein sources throughout the day. Now is a good time to dispel the old myth that you must combine complementary plant proteins in one meal to get a complete protein. Research shows that as long as you eat a variety of plant protein sources throughout the day, you'll be fine.

Edamame, quinoa, amaranth, and chia and hemp seeds are all complete proteins—meaning they contain all the essential amino acids.

OMEGA-3 FATTY ACIDS Omega-3s supply your body with energy and play a vital role in heart, lung, and immune function, as well as hormone production. The three main omega-3s are eicosapentaenoic acid (EPA) and docosahexaenoic acid (DHA), which are found in oily fish and seafood, including anchovies, salmon, sardines, mackerel, and sablefish; and alpha-linolenic acid (ALA), which is found in plant foods such as walnuts, flaxseed, chia seeds, and some plant oils.

EPA and DHA have been researched extensively and are associated with a number of potential health benefits including better infant health and development outcomes; a lower risk for heart disease, Alzheimer's disease, and age-related macular degeneration; and better arthritis management.

Though your body can convert some ALA into EPA, and then DHA, the process is inefficient. If you are not regularly eating fatty fish, you might consider supplementation with guidance from a health professional. Choose a high-quality fish oil supplement that contains both DHA and EPA; or for a vegan option, go with algae-based supplements.

VITAMIN B$_{12}$ B$_{12}$ is important for healthy red-blood-cell formation, DNA synthesis, and our central nervous system, among other functions. This vital nutrient is found exclusively in animal foods and a limited number of fortified plant foods. It's one of the few nutrients that you cannot easily get from plants. Plus, as we age, we tend to absorb less B$_{12}$ from the foods we eat.

If you eat meat, fish, and dairy foods regularly, you are less likely to have issues with getting enough B$_{12}$. But if you're following a 100 percent plant-based diet, you'll likely need a B$_{12}$ supplement. You can also be diligent about eating vegan foods fortified with B$_{12}$, including breakfast cereals, some plant milk, and nutritional yeast.

Note: You might see that some types of seaweed contain B$_{12}$. It's important to know that seaweed alone is not a reliable or sufficient way to meet your B$_{12}$ needs.

IRON Iron is essential for transporting oxygen to every tissue of the body and is important for growth and development, as well as for making some hormones. It's abundant and better absorbed from foods of animal origin that contain heme iron. Switching to an all-plant diet can mean paying a bit more attention to the iron-rich plants you put on the plate.

Foods like beans and lentils, cooked spinach, and pumpkin or hemp seeds are sources of non-heme iron. But so is dark chocolate, which delivers almost 40 percent of the daily value for iron in just three ounces! Be sure to also check the label of your favorite cereal, because some fortified ones contain a full day's supply of iron.

Tip: To absorb more iron from plant-based sources, combine your iron-rich plant foods with a source of vitamin C. Vitamin C has been shown to improve absorption of iron, making it more available to your body. Thankfully, this can be done deliciously (see the Simplest Green Smoothie, page 213)! You might combine black beans and salsa, lentils with red bell peppers, or cooked spinach with tomatoes. Have fun creating other dynamic duos to enhance absorption.

CALCIUM As the key structural component of bones and teeth, it's no surprise that calcium is the most abundant nutrient in the body. It's also important for heart, muscle, and nerve function. Dairy foods such as yogurt, milk, and cheese are rich in calcium, but there are other ways to get it.

Calcium is often added to foods such as plant milk and orange juice. Calcium-fortified orange juice and soy milk often contain more calcium per cup than a cup of whole milk. But keep in mind it may or may not be as readily absorbed.

Cooked edamame, fortified breakfast cereal, and tofu formed with calcium sulfate are all good sources of calcium too. Cooked leafy greens, such as spinach, turnip greens, and kale, and some nuts and many seeds also have calcium. An ounce of almonds delivers 6 percent of the daily value for calcium. And if you're a fan of poppy seeds, they are great to stock. Just one tablespoon contains 10 percent of the daily value for calcium. And sesame seeds are close behind, providing 7 percent of the daily value in just one tablespoon.

If seafood is part of your plant-forward approach, sardines or canned pink salmon with the soft bones are also convenient ways to get your calcium.

ZINC Zinc is important for immune health, making proteins and DNA, proper wound healing, and enabling our senses of taste and smell. It is abundant in and easily absorbed from seafood, pork, and other animal foods, so if you eat a standard American diet, it's usually pretty easy to meet your zinc needs. To that point, overt zinc deficiency is rare in the general healthy population.

If you're OK with seafood, oysters are well known as the top source for zinc, providing well over 100 percent of the daily value in a three-ounce serving. But if you're like most people, oysters are not a common food in your diet. Luckily, other seafood, beef, and pork are also very high in zinc, with more than 25 percent of the daily value in three ounces.

But if you don't eat meat or seafood, you'll need to include plant sources of the nutrient. Luckily, there are lots. Some of the heavy hitters include white beans, pumpkin seeds, and fortified cereals. Cashews, chickpeas, and oatmeal are other top sources. Keep these top of mind, and find ways to add them to your meals daily.

It's notable that vegetarians sometimes need as much as 50 percent more zinc than the recommended daily value because plants often contain binders—called phytates—that make zinc less available. To add more to your day, in addition to the foods mentioned above, you might consider soaking your beans, grains, and seeds to let them sprout. This helps unlock the zinc so that it is more available for your body to absorb. Also, it's a good time to mention that it's easier to absorb more zinc from leavened grains, such as bread, than from those without leavening.

ARE FORTIFIED OR ENRICHED FOODS OK TO INCLUDE?

Yes. Enriched foods are those in which nutrients have been added back to replace ones that may have been lost during processing. This is common with foods like white rice and whole wheat bread.

Fortified foods also have added nutrients but may or may not have contained the nutrients originally—such as in calcium-fortified orange juice or certain plant milk and cereals.

One thing you might have noticed is that fortified cereals show up often on lists of foods to help meet your nutrient needs. This is because fortification helps close many gaps, and sometimes the nutrients are better absorbed from these foods.

DOES SPROUTING BEANS, NUTS, AND GRAINS MAKE THEM HEALTHIER?

Generally speaking, yes! Though it varies by the grain, bean, or nut, safely soaking and sprouting some foods can help increase the availability of certain nutrients including protein, soluble fiber, vitamin C, folate, and antioxidants. Sprouting may also help improve the digestibility of certain grains. It's thought that the sprouting process helps predigest or partially digest the grain while simultaneously increasing enzymes (phytase and amylase) that may help with overall digestion.

The exact effects depend on the type of food (grains, beans, nuts), the nutrients in the food, and the sprouting process—it's not the same across the board. For example, folate has been shown to be four times higher in sprouted wheat pita. And one study found that sprouted brown rice may help with blood sugar control and promote better blood lipid profiles for people with diabetes.

Importantly, sprouting might also help reduce the anti-nutrients in some foods that make it difficult to absorb other nutrients such as calcium and iron. For example, sprouting millet boosts the availability of iron and improves calcium and manganese accessibility as well.

Bottom Line: Getting proper nutrition takes planning whether you are eating meat or not. Once you know the possible gaps, it's easy to plan meals that work for you and your family.

But remember, if you take the plant-forward approach and regularly include some of the animal sources mentioned, it becomes easier to meet your nutrient needs.

Now let's talk about supplementation. It's possible to get most nutrients from food, but no diet is perfect. Additionally, some nutrients, like omega-3s and vitamin D, are difficult to get from food sources alone, since there are few options that provide them in large enough quantities. Be sure to discuss your specific needs with your health-care provider. If you don't find yourself eating the foods mentioned, or believe you have symptoms of deficiencies or inadequate intake of any specific vitamin, check with your health-care provider for guidance.

PLANT-FORWARD PRINCIPLES

Adopting a plant-forward approach may be one of the easiest things you'll do to improve your health. And there are just two simple principles:

1. Shift your mindset. In the South, where I live, you'll find meat-and-three plates at many restaurants. Most menus list the meatiest entrées at the top, with one or two vegetarian options at the bottom or on a special menu. We are used to seeing meat options first.

I'm asking you to flip that on its head. Instead of thinking of what can go with chicken for dinner, first think about the vegetables you'll have, then maybe how meat might enhance the flavor or be an optional or smaller part of the meal. This shift will take time, but don't worry—I have some tips to help you with the transition later in this chapter.

2. Keep an open mind. A key to success is starting with the plant foods you enjoy most. But to keep it interesting, be open to exploring and discovering new ones, or new ways to prepare the ones you already eat.

This book combines both familiar and new-to-you ingredients and recipes from all over the world. The aim is to provide accessible options to help you start exploring the infinite ways plants can grace your plate. So let's dig in!

PLANT-FORWARD FAQS

When starting any new eating plan, please consult your personal health-care provider for guidance on what works best for you. Here are a few general questions that commonly crop up.

WHY IS THIS BOOK CALLED *THE PLANT LOVE KITCHEN*? Every recipe in this book contains plants! Though there are foods from animal sources, plants are the center of attention. You'll find recipes celebrating different fruits, vegetables, grains, legumes, nuts, and more. Look out for fun facts and nutrition tidbits throughout too.

WHAT DO YOU MEAN BY CHANGING YOUR MINDSET? Plant-forward eating is more about the way you cook and how you *think* about what you put on your plate, and less about what you can and can't have, following a rigid schedule, or adhering to arbitrary diet phases to get to an imaginary finish line.

Start where you are and go at your own pace. Take it slow and steady, go back and forth, or move full steam ahead.

WHY FOLLOW A PLANT-FORWARD WAY OF EATING? It's nourishing. It's enjoyable. And eating more plants tends to make you feel good and help you lead a healthier, happier, better-quality life.

With all there is to gain, the fact remains that nine in 10 adults miss the fruit and vegetable mark each day. So we have a lot of work to do!

WILL THERE BE PLANT-FORWARD OPTIONS WHEN I EAT OUT? In most major metropolitan areas, vegan and vegetarian options are becoming more and more common—even at chain and popular restaurants. Chefs are aware of the growing demand for plant-forward options and are making more choices available. Servers are also familiar with what makes a dish vegan or vegetarian, so they can properly guide guests in their meal choices.

But feel free to get creative. Ask for a double portion of vegetables, request extra peppers on a pizza or in a stir-fry, order a veggie-rich appetizer like soup or salad, or simply accept that some meals will contain fewer plants, and that's OK!

DO I HAVE TO EAT DIFFERENTLY DURING THE HOLIDAYS? Not really. If you are transitioning to a more plant-based lifestyle, the holidays can bring up lots of questions. If you're asking yourself: Do I need to change our traditions? Do we need to change our holiday turkey to a tofu loaf? Can I eat my auntie's green bean casserole that I really love? These are all valid questions.

And the good news is that following a plant-forward way of eating doesn't require you to choose or change those traditions at all. Festive meals are a part of life and don't have to be eliminated. There's freedom in knowing that, which hopefully helps eliminate any angst that might come up around the holidays.

If you are going in the other direction—transitioning from a vegan or vegetarian diet to one that's less restrictive—taking the plant-forward leap might offer some relief. It means you can enjoy the greens made with a little bit of meat for flavoring without asking your family to make a separate batch for you.

With the plant-forward mindset shift, you might find that you reach for a plate of sides and may or may not feel the desire to have lots of meat anyway.

MAKING YOUR PLATE

There are many different ways to compose a plate, from aiming for specific macronutrient (carbohydrate, protein, fat) percentages following the U.S. Department of Agriculture and U.S. Department of Health and Human Services' *Dietary Guidelines for Americans* to the plate method—which suggests filling half the plate with fruits and vegetables, a quarter with protein, and a quarter with your favorite starchy vegetable or carbohydrate such as rice or another grain—and everything in between.

My approach is more fluid. As a registered dietitian nutritionist, I focus first on foods that satisfy and that I enjoy. Nutrition is important for our overall health, so when creating a balanced meal, I loosely follow the plate method.

If you're wondering about calories, I don't count them.

In pursuing a plant-forward mindset, I encourage you to keep it simple. Think first about what plants to add to the plate and then how to make them taste great. This may mean that some days you just want to eat a big plate of vegetables for dinner—which I applaud. But I also caution you to ensure balance whenever possible.

One of the biggest mistakes I see when people transition to eat more plants is that they eliminate meat without finding any replacement. The result is hunger and quickly giving up. It's important to include a good protein source, healthy fats, and fiber so that you feel satisfied. That may mean including chickpeas or lentils as one of the vegetables on that plate.

It will take time to figure out what works for you, but with a little trial and error, you'll get in the groove.

The Plant Love Journey

The Plant Love Kitchen will help you shift your mindset to put plants first. You'll discover delicious and easy ways to upgrade your diet with more plant-based meals. All without rigid rules or the need to eliminate any specific foods. *The only foods off-limits are those you don't like or are allergic to!*

The good news is that when you adopt a plant-forward way of eating, you can start wherever you are with whatever you have on hand. It's a gradual shift that can eventually become second nature and possibly even preferred. Here are some tips to help you get started.

TRANSITIONING TO A PLANT-FORWARD WAY OF EATING

FIND YOUR WHY. Assess the reasons you're exploring a plant-forward diet. This is an important place to start because it will help find and steer your motivation.

Are you aiming for a healthier heart, a happier gut, longevity, or increased energy, or to do your part to help the environment? Or is it simply a matter of preference? Maybe you never really liked eating meat, or you're going through a phase and want a way to expand your palate beyond beans and rice.

Your why is valid and can change over time.

SHIFT YOUR MINDSET. This change in mindset is a cornerstone of plant-forward eating. By centering plants on the plate, you'll begin thinking differently about how you shop for groceries, how you scan restaurant menus, and even how you plan picnics, parties, and cookouts.

It's a bit misleading to list this one as a single step. You'll do this throughout your journey to add more plants to your plate and maybe eventually arrive at the point where you automatically think of animal protein as being an optional side or a way to add flavor to a meal, versus being the star.

KEEP YOUR FAVORITES. A plant-forward way of eating doesn't require you to completely give up anything. Instead, it opens the door to explore new possibilities. A plant-forward lifestyle means you can start the day with a tofu scramble for breakfast and end the day with your grandma's collard greens cooked with ham hocks if you want. If you love your traditional or cultural foods that contain meat, you can still enjoy them without a second thought.

There's freedom in flexibility. Eating some meat here and there doesn't completely thwart your health journey. Being and eating well is not black or white. Plant-forward eating lets you deliciously embrace the gray.

REPLACE RATHER THAN ELIMINATE. This might be one of the most important steps in successfully transitioning to a plant-forward way of eating. If you simply stop eating meat at dinner, you might find yourself awake and hungry at 2 a.m.

The Plant Love Kitchen will help you reinvent dinner (breakfast, lunch, and snacks too) to include plant protein, fiber, and healthy fats so that you are both nourished and satisfied. This might mean adding white beans to your favorite pasta dish or roasted chickpeas to your big salad if you're not eating animal protein that night.

BUILD HABITS, NOT ONE BIG END-OF-THE-ROAD GOAL. Start small. Make changes over time based on what works for you. The transition is iterative, intuitive, and forgiving. Start by thinking about the smallest possible change you can make, such as adding vegetables to breakfast. You might start by folding leftover roasted vegetables into an omelet and eventually go all in with my Chickpea Breakfast Scramble (page 84).

It takes time to build healthy-habit pathways. And it may take longer than the 21 or 60 days you may have heard touted by eating programs before. And that's OK. It's about progress, not perfection.

Instead of overhauling your kitchen overnight, which can be overwhelming, start small. Target one meal a day, or even one meal a week, where you shift your plate in the plant direction.

Deciding to expand your palate can be a bit intimidating. But think of how you might break it down into tiny steps to get started.

Try This: The next time you shop for groceries, add one new plant food to your list. It can be one vegetable, fruit, or grain—even an herb or a spice—that you've never tried before. If you decide to add turmeric, that's your first step. Finding a recipe to make with it is the second. (I suggest the Quick Coconut Chickpea Stew on page 164.) Making the recipe completes the cycle, and you get to do it all over again with a new food next time.

PLAN AHEAD. Take a few minutes each week to set yourself up for success. The next chapter includes tips for meal prep and planning, but it's important to remember that great meals won't just happen. You have to plan for them. But it doesn't have to be difficult.

Note: Take the easy route sometimes. You don't have to make everything from scratch to form successful habits. Canned beans are fine—and we'll use lots in these recipes.

KEEP IT INTERESTING. Look to cuisines from across the globe to stay inspired and to experiment with new ideas and flavors. Many cultures take a plant-forward approach, so there's no lack of inspiration out there!

MEAL PLANS

In my one-to-one nutrition coaching, I meet my clients wherever they are. No judgment. *The Plant Love Kitchen* meal plans do just that. These examples include three different options to try based on your comfort level. As you become more comfortable, you can add more meatless meals. You can make swaps and stay on each one for as long as you like!

Each plan includes breakfast, lunch, and dinner suggestions, plus snack ideas and extras (such as yogurt with berries). But these are simply suggestions. Be sure to add your own spin, mix and match your favorites, eat out, and, by all means, use leftovers!

THE PLANT LOVE KITCHEN MEAL PLAN 1

This is a great place to start if you are currently eating meat, fish, or poultry two or more times per day. Plan 1 will introduce you to the idea of having and enjoying meals without meat and even some that are 100 percent plant-based.

	Monday	Tuesday	Wednesday	Thursday	Friday	Saturday	Sunday
Breakfast	Make-Ahead Spinach Breakfast Wraps *Page 83* Tea	Make-Ahead Spinach Breakfast Wraps *Page 83* Tea	Nutty Caramelized Banana and Steel-Cut Oats *Page 87* Creamy Cardamom and Cashew Coffee *Page 215*	Peach Almond Baked Oatmeal *Page 91* Simplest Green Smoothie *Page 213*	Peach Almond Baked Oatmeal *Page 91* Simplest Green Smoothie *Page 213*	Baked Eggs and Greens *Page 81* Orange juice	Caramelized Pears With Walnuts and Yogurt *Page 90* Tea
Lunch	Black Bean and Spinach Quesadillas *Page 137* Watermelon Salad With Honey-Lime Vinaigrette *Page 135*	Black Bean and Spinach Quesadillas *Page 137* Watermelon Salad With Honey-Lime Vinaigrette *Page 135*	Pesto Chickpea Bowls *Page 131* Orange wedges	Tomato, Olive, and Arugula Frittata *Page 159* Fresh berries	Tomato, Olive, and Arugula Frittata *Page 159* Fresh berries	Mushroom Cheesesteak *Page 139* Fries Salad greens with vinaigrette	Mushroom Cheesesteak *Page 139* Fries Salad greens with vinaigrette
Dinner	Blended Chicken and Mushroom Meatballs *Page 148* Honey Pepper Broccoli *Page 190* Rice	Sheet Pan Fajitas *Page 178* Blender Salsa *Page 71*	Black Beans and Cheese Grits *Page 155*	Mushroom and Lentil Bolognese *Page 154* Crusty bread	Black Bean and Cheddar Burgers *Page 133* Fries	Rosemary-Roasted Salmon and Grapes *Page 161* Honey Nut–Roasted Brussels Sprouts *Page 205*	Spinach and Ricotta Linguine *Page 171* Cherry Almond Crisp *Page 221*
Snacks	Fruit and Oat Bars *Page 99*	Fruit and Oat Bars *Page 99*	Rosemary-Roasted Walnuts *Page 103*	Rosemary-Roasted Walnuts *Page 103*	Peanut Chili Crunch Popcorn *Page 107*	My Chai Concentrate *Page 211*	Brown Butter Pistachio Cookies *Page 225*

THE PLANT LOVE KITCHEN MEAL PLAN 2

Ready to really up your plant game? This meal plan will help you do it. Here, plants take center stage on most nights of the week. Plus, the snacks are 100 percent plant-based, and most can be made ahead to fill any hungry gaps during the day.

	Monday	Tuesday	Wednesday	Thursday	Friday	Saturday	Sunday
Breakfast	Peach Almond Baked Oatmeal *Page 91* Creamy Cardamom and Cashew Coffee *Page 215*	Peach Almond Baked Oatmeal *Page 91* Creamy Cardamom and Cashew Coffee *Page 215*	Savory Quinoa Breakfast Bowls *Page 85* Walnut Breakfast Patties *Page 86* Tea	Savory Quinoa Breakfast Bowls *Page 85* Tea	Blueberry Buttermilk Oat Muffins *Page 93* Greek yogurt Tea	Blueberry Buttermilk Oat Muffins *Page 93* Greek yogurt Tea	Baked Eggs and Greens *Page 81* Orange juice
Lunch	Pesto Chickpea Bowls *Page 131*	Pesto Chickpea Bowls *Page 131*	Roasted Shrimp, Pineapple, and Pepper Tacos *Page 183*	Mushroom Ricotta Toast *Page 121*	Black Bean and Spinach Quesadillas *Page 137* Watermelon Salad With Honey-Lime Vinaigrette *Page 135*	Black Bean and Spinach Quesadillas *Page 137* Watermelon Salad With Honey-Lime Vinaigrette *Page 135*	Cauliflower and Avocado Tacos *Page 157* Blender Salsa *Page 71* Tortilla Chips Corn bread
Dinner	Spicy BBQ Tofu Lettuce Cups *Page 175*	Roasted Shrimp, Pineapple, and Pepper Tacos *Page 183*	Black Beans and Cheese Grits *Page 155*	Lentil-Stuffed Peppers *Page 185*	Tomato, Olive, and Arugula Frittata *Page 159* Maple Miso–Glazed Sweet Potatoes *Page 199*	Mushroom Cheese-steak *Page 139* Fries Salad greens with vinaigrette	Spinach and Ricotta Linguine *Page 171* Cherry Almond Crisp *Page 221*
Snacks	Fruit and Oat Bars *Page 99*	Fruit and Oat Bars *Page 99*	Creamy Banana-Nut Smoothie *Page 219*	Creamy Banana-Nut Smoothie *Page 219*	Peanut Chili Crunch Popcorn *Page 107*	BBQ-Roasted Black-Eyed Peas *Page 101*	BBQ-Roasted Black-Eyed Peas *Page 101*

THE PLANT LOVE KITCHEN MEAL PLAN 3

Plants are now your first thought when it comes to meal planning. You're ready to enjoy meatless meals on most or all days of the week. This plan has recipes that can be made 100 percent plant-based whenever you're ready.

	Monday	Tuesday	Wednesday	Thursday	Friday	Saturday	Sunday
Breakfast	Make-Ahead Spinach Breakfast Wraps *Page 83* Simplest Green Smoothie *Page 213*	Make-Ahead Spinach Breakfast Wraps *Page 83* Simplest Green Smoothie *Page 213*	Nutty Caramelized Banana and Steel-Cut Oats *Page 87* Creamy Cardamom and Cashew Coffee *Page 215*	Fully Loaded Breakfast Cookies *Page 95* Vegan or Greek yogurt	Fully Loaded Breakfast Cookies *Page 95* Vegan or Greek yogurt	Chickpea Breakfast Scramble *Page 84* Creamy Cardamom and Cashew Coffee *Page 215*	Chickpea Breakfast Scramble *Page 84* Orange juice
Lunch	Brown Rice and Cabbage Crunch Salad *Page 117* Crispy tofu	Smashed Chickpea Salad Sandwich *Page 127*	Smashed Chickpea Salad Sandwich *Page 127*	Socca With Sautéed Vegetables *Page 181*	Quick Coconut Chickpea Stew *Page 164* Rice	Black Bean and Spinach Quesadillas *Page 137* Roasted Carrot Soup *Page 141*	Herbed Cauliflower and White Bean Soup *Page 126* Vegan grilled cheese
Dinner	Winter Squash Red Curry *Page 165*	Pinto Bean Cakes With Avocado Salsa *Page 167*	Spicy BBQ Tofu Lettuce Cups *Page 175* Kale Slaw With Peanut Dressing *Page 179*	Spicy BBQ Tofu Lettuce Cups *Page 175* Kale Slaw With Peanut Dressing *Page 179*	Black Bean and Cheddar Burgers *Page 133* Fries	Creamy Roasted Red Pepper Pasta *Page 149*	Peanut Stew *Page 145* Rice
Snacks	BBQ-Roasted Black-Eyed Peas *Page 101*	Creamy Banana Nut-Smoothie *Page 219*	Creamy Banana Nut-Smoothie *Page 219*	Fruit and Oat Bars *Page 99*	Blueberry Cream Pops *Page 209*	Sweet and Salty Pepita Granola *Page 111*	Cocoa Almond Truffles *Page 229*

The Plant Love Kitchen

We've established that plant-forward means you don't have to eliminate any food or food group. Focusing on plants *most* of the time means having the flexibility to consume dairy or other foods without worry. It's freeing and allows you to eat intuitively, enjoy your favorite foods, and choose what's best for your body at any given time.

But this *is* a new way of thinking. And it may be prudent to put some things in place to help create an environment for success.

Cooking a new way can be intimidating. From the many messages about the best ways to maintain a plant-based diet to pressure to buy this or that expensive gadget or the latest organic "superfood," there is a lot of food and nutrition noise out there. Just the idea of getting started the "right way" can seem overwhelming.

This is especially true if you don't feel like cooking most days or you typically eat out but want to work toward making more meals at home for better health. I understand. And I hope you'll be relieved to know that making the adjustment toward a plant-forward lifestyle is actually quite simple. In this chapter, I break down my practical tips and tidbits to help you find your way through this journey with ease—from lists for stocking your fridge and pantry to guides on how to cook staple ingredients.

When starting anything new, it's important to set yourself up for success. Here are a few steps to mentally prepare for this change.

1. **Start.** Acknowledge where you are and take small steps to gradually eat more plants and less meat. This might be as simple as trying a new spice the next time you go grocery shopping.

2. **Prioritize.** Begin with the plant foods you enjoy and then branch out.

3. **Embrace imperfection.** Though plants are always in focus, adopting a plant-forward way of eating lets you enjoy what you eat with ease since there are no strict rules or regimens.

4. **Design.** Organize your kitchen and pantry—and your mindset—as a positive space for experimenting with new foods, flavors, and ways of thinking.

Now let's get into the specifics. Read on for the tools you need to prepare your plant-forward kitchen!

STOCK YOUR FRIDGE, FREEZER, AND PANTRY

Have these ingredients and you'll be well prepared for plant-forward eating. Don't forget to look before you shop: Many of these ingredients are things you may already have on hand.

PLANT-POWERED REFRIGERATOR

- Bell peppers
- Brussels sprouts
- Broccoli
- Cabbage
- Carrots
- Cauliflower
- Chutneys
- Dairy, nondairy, or plant milk (soy, oat, almond, cashew, pea protein, hemp, or rice)
- Fresh fruit including citrus (lemons, limes, oranges), stone fruit (cherries, peaches, plums), grapes, berries, apples, and pears
- Fresh fruit jams
- Fresh herbs (basil, cilantro, mint, parsley)
- Green beans
- Green onions or scallions
- Homemade pesto (see page 72)
- Kimchi*
- Leafy greens (arugula, collards, kale, spinach)
- Salsa
- Toasted sesame oil
- Tofu and tempeh
- White (or shiro) miso paste*

Optional:
- Butter (or vegan butter)
- Cheese (Parmesan, cotija, Swiss, cheddar, or goat)
- Chicken or turkey
- Fresh fish (cod, salmon, trout, flounder, or pollock)
- Greek yogurt**
- Buttermilk
- Shellfish (shrimp, crab, or scallops)

* Check it out: Shop your local, international, or Asian markets for foods like miso and kimchi. Some well-stocked major supermarkets also carry these in the produce department or in a refrigerated endcap.

** I use full-fat yogurt in my recipes; feel free to use lower-fat versions if you prefer.

PLANT-POWERED FREEZER
- Frozen cooked rice and other grains
- Frozen fish, chicken, turkey, etc.
- Frozen fruit
- Frozen vegetables including leftover or pre-chopped peppers and onions

PLANT-POWERED PANTRY
Produce:
- Avocados
- Bananas
- Cherry or grape tomatoes
- Garlic
- Mangoes
- Onions (red, sweet, white, and yellow)
- Potatoes (white, red)
- Roma or beefsteak and other slicing tomatoes
- Shallots
- Sweet potatoes

Spices:

(At minimum, stock up on these spices—but there's always room for more!)

- Bay leaves
- Black pepper
- Cardamom
- Cayenne pepper
- Chili powder (ancho, chipotle, etc.)
- Cinnamon
- Coriander
- Cumin
- Curry powder
- Dried herbs (Italian seasoning, rosemary, basil, parsley, thyme, oregano)
- Garlic powder
- Ginger powder
- Mustard powder and seeds
- Nutmeg
- Onion powder
- Paprika (smoked and sweet)
- Red pepper flakes, crushed
- Salt
- Spice blends (berbere, garam masala, five-spice powder, za'atar)
- Turmeric
- Vanilla and other extracts

Canned and Packaged Goods:

- Arrowroot powder
- Baking powder
- Baking soda
- Brown sugar
- Canned crushed or diced tomatoes
- Canned peas, beans, lentils
- Canned stewed whole tomatoes
- Canned tomato paste
- Cocoa powder
- Coconut sugar
- Coffee

- Cornstarch
- Date sugar
- Dried beans (pinto, kidney, and black)
- Dried chickpeas, pigeon peas, and cowpeas (black-eyed and crowder)
- Dried lentils (red, green, brown, black, beluga)
- Dried peas (yellow and green whole or split)
- Flax and flaxseed meal
- Flour (all-purpose, almond, chickpea, or tapioca)
- Gluten- and grain-free or legume-based pasta (chickpea, lentil)
- Honey
- Maple syrup
- Nut and seed butters* (peanut, almond, cashew, sunflower)
- Nuts (almonds, peanuts, pecans, pistachios, walnuts)
- Oats (quick-cooking, traditional or old-fashioned, steel-cut)
- Oil (extra-virgin olive, avocado, coconut)
- Quinoa
- Rice (white, brown, wild)
- Seeds (chia, hemp, pumpkin, sesame, sunflower)
- Tea (black, green, oolong, rooibos, hibiscus, other herbal)

Condiments:
- Chili crisp oil
- Chili paste
- Coconut aminos
- Curry paste
- Hot sauce
- Ketchup
- Mustard (Dijon, hot, brown, whole, yellow)
- Soy sauce
- Tamari
- Vinegar (balsamic, apple cider, red wine, white wine, champagne, unseasoned rice)
- Worcestershire sauce (regular or vegan)

* These are listed as pantry staples but should be stored in the refrigerator or freezer for a longer shelf life.

STOCK YOUR KITCHEN

Set yourself up for success with the right kitchen tools. Maintaining a plant-forward lifestyle doesn't require a ton of fancy gadgets—no special juice makers or spiralizers here! But investing in a few pieces of equipment can help trim prep time and instill confidence in the kitchen.

Check these off for a well-equipped kitchen:

Appliances:
- Air fryer (optional)
- Electric pressure cooker (optional for pressure-cooking beans)
- Food processor (for making energy bites and quickly chopping vegetables)
- Hand mixer (for quick breads and whipping cream)
- High-powered blender (for making nut butters and plant milks)
- Stick or immersion blender (for pureeing soups and sauces)
- Slow cooker (optional)
- Toaster oven (optional)

Kitchen Basics:
- 5-to-7-quart Dutch oven
- 8-by-8-inch and 9-by-13-inch casserole dishes and baking pans
- 10- and 12-inch sauté pans and/or cast-iron skillet
- Assorted mason jars with lids
- Box-style cheese grater
- Chef's knife
- Citrus juicer
- Colander
- Cooling racks
- Cutting boards (wood, bamboo, or recycled plastic)
- Dishcloths and napkins
- Electric or stovetop kettle
- Glass or silicone storage containers with lids
- Heavy-duty baking sheets (large and small)
- Kitchen scale (for measuring baking ingredients)
- Kitchen shears

- Knife sharpener
- Loaf pans
- Measuring spoons
- Mixing bowls (three or four)
- Muffin tin
- Nut milk bag or cheesecloth (for making homemade plant milk)
- Paring knife
- Potato masher
- Rasp grater (Microplane for zesting citrus and grating garlic, hard cheeses, and spices)
- Rolling pin
- Serrated or bread knife
- Silicone baking mat and/or parchment paper
- Silicone spatulas
- Tongs
- Wet and dry measuring cup
- Wire mesh strainers (small, medium, and large)
- Whisks (large and small)
- Wooden spoons

Drawer Gadgets:
- Can opener
- Cherry pitter (also works for pitting olives)
- Vegetable peeler and julienne slicer
- Wine opener or corkscrew

WAYS TO BUILD A PLANT-FORWARD MEAL

Putting plants front and center on your plate can be an adjustment, but it gets easier with practice. And there is no one way. I promise, plant-forward meals are just as satisfying and filling when made the right way. And it doesn't have to be all or nothing either—you can make an entirely plant-based dinner, or simply add more plants to your typical plate, like tossing chickpeas and tomatoes into your favorite pasta dish.

Don't know where to start? Consider these easy meal ideas as your first options:

1. Make a veggie-rich stew and serve it over grains. (Try the Peanut Stew, page 145.).

2. Whip up a lentil or bean soup and serve it with crusty bread. (Try the Herbed Cauliflower and White Bean Soup, page 126.)

3. Sauté vegetables. Cover them with eggs or a plant-based egg substitute to make a frittata. Serve it with a salad or bread. (Try the Chickpea Breakfast Scramble, page 84.)

4. Try tofu in place of shrimp, chicken, or pork in rice dishes or appetizers. (Try the Spicy BBQ Tofu Lettuce Cups, page 175.)

5. Add white beans to pasta along with plenty of tomatoes and/or greens.

6. Make a burger from beans or quinoa. Add fries to the meal, because burgers and fries are part of the plant-forward way. (Try the Black Bean and Cheddar Burgers, page 133.)

7. Simply sear marinated tempeh or tofu and serve it with chimichurri, pesto, or another vegetable sauce.

8. Make a veggie plate. Choose your favorites for an epic veggie feast. I'd go for the Crispy Okra (page 189), Pan-Seared Beans and Greens (page 201), and Maple Miso–Glazed Sweet Potatoes (page 199).

FLAVOR BUILDERS

MAKING YOUR MEALS TASTE GREAT

Flavor-Intensifying Techniques

Though we often think about what ingredient to add to a dish to bring on more flavor, *the way* your meal is cooked cannot be ignored. Culinary techniques can amp up the flavor of the simplest recipe. Look for these buzzwords as a signal for flavor, and add them to your cooking routine where you can:

Blooming: The process of cooking dry spices in oil until fragrant but not brown helps release and boost the flavor of the spices while simultaneously infusing the flavor throughout the dish.

Broiling: This oft-overlooked way of preparing vegetables, fruits, and fish is the closest you might get to grilling indoors—especially if you have a gas oven. Broiling helps brown vegetables, fish, and other foods, which in turn adds flavor.

Caramelizing: Mushrooms get sweeter when their natural sugars are allowed to caramelize. (Try them with my Mushroom Cheesesteak, page 139.) And onions slow-cooked until they are smoky and unbelievably sweet is one of life's best treats. Use caramelized onions for topping pizza and sandwiches, or add them to dips for a deep, rich flavor.

Deglazing the pan: Never skip this step. Adding broth, water, wine, or another liquid to the pan after searing vegetables, fruit, tofu, or meat helps lift the flavorful brown bits from the bottom of your pan to add loads of flavor to your dish. Those brown bits (known as fond) are a key part of the flavor profile. Add the liquid, watch it sizzle, then scrape all the bits from the pan with a wooden spoon. This technique also makes for easier cleanup!

Grilling: An ancient practice, open-fire roasting or grilling adds smoky flavor—often in very little time. What's great is that vegetables grill up quickly and don't leave as much of a mess as meat.

Pan-searing: Cooking mushrooms, vegetables, fish, poultry, or meat in a hot pan on the stovetop triggers the Maillard reaction (aka browning), which causes the proteins and sugars to come together for caramelized, complex, and aromatic flavor.

Reducing a sauce: Allowing water to evaporate and a sauce to thicken concentrates and boosts the sauce's final flavor. If you're making a glaze, thickening the glaze will help it stick to your food.

Roasting: Cooking vegetables in a hot oven imparts a smoky, sweet flavor, thanks to the caramelized edges and tender centers. There are infinite flavor combinations to try when it comes to seasoning your veggies, and it starts with the simplest coating of oil, salt, and pepper.

Toasting: Just as toasting a piece of bread can help enliven the malty flavor of the slice, heating whole spices and dried herbs in a dry skillet can awaken flavors. Simply toast your spices in a dry skillet over medium-low heat until fragrant and lightly golden but not scorched.

FLAVORFUL INGREDIENTS

Sometimes, all you need is one extra ingredient to amp up your meal's flavor. If you're reluctant about eating more plants, these simple adjustments can make all the difference. Give these a try:

Add acid. White and red wine can brighten a dish, while sherry and marsala add depth. All types of vinegars and citrus juices and zest add balance and lift flavors. Often when you think a dish is missing something, a splash of vinegar or citrus juice—like a squeeze of lemon—will rescue it.

Bring on the broth. Instead of water, use homemade or high-quality vegetable or chicken broth to cook grains or as the base for a soup or sauce.

Season well. Salt and pepper are just the start. Stock a variety of spices to amplify the flavor of your meals. Just be sure to refresh your spice stash once or twice a year—spices lose their flavor over time.

Get saucy. Salsa, chutney, chimichurri, pesto, and other condiments are easy to make with fresh ingredients and just a knife or blender at home. You can also buy these—but be sure to check the quality and ingredients.

Feel the brine. Olives of all types, pickles, capers, and other brined ingredients add tangy flavor to salads, sauces, and more.

Sweeten the deal. Peppers such as shishito, ancho, Calabrian, guajillo,

piquillo, and Peppadew can add sweet or mild heat to dishes—plus a pop of color.

Turn up the heat. Add some spice with hot chili peppers, horseradish or wasabi, hot mustard, hot sauce, or chili crisp oil.

Roast garlic. Simply wrap a whole bulb (with the ends chopped off and papery skin removed), covered in olive oil, in tinfoil and roast at 400°F for 30 to 40 minutes. Once cool enough to handle, squeeze the cloves out of the bulb into a bowl, add oil from the foil, and stir until a paste forms. Keep the resulting roasted garlic paste in the refrigerator in a sealed container to add a rich, sweet garlic flavor to your dishes and sauces. You can even smear it on toast and eat it just as is!

Go bold. Add tanginess and color with pomegranate arils or fresh cilantro or other fresh herbs.

Think whole. Use whole spices such as freshly grated nutmeg and cracked cardamom pods if you can find them. Check your local farmers market, where spices are often significantly less expensive than what you'll find in the supermarket.

Get smoky. Add ancho chili peppers, smoked paprika, or smoked salt to dishes for a hint of smoky flavor when you are not able to use a grill.

GET TO KNOW UMAMI

Once upon a time, you may have learned that there are four core tastes: sweet, salty, bitter, and sour. But there is a fifth one—no, it's not new, and it's arguably my favorite. That's umami. Umami might be described as a deep savory flavor or meatiness.

When you replace or eat less meat, you might miss the savory depth of flavor it can provide. Here are some ways to add that flavor back to your meals using all plant-based ingredients.

FOODS THAT DELIVER ULTIMATE UMAMI FLAVOR:

- Miso
- Tomatoes
- Smoked paprika
- Nutritional yeast (aka nooch)
- Fermented black beans
- Seaweed
- Dried and fresh mushrooms
- Mushroom broth
- Soy sauce
- Tamari
- Coconut aminos
- Parmesan rind (though not plant-based, this is another way to impart savory flavor into soups and stews)

MORE ABOUT MISO

Don't put your miso in a corner of the fridge and forget about it. Pull it out for dressings, sauces, and, yes, miso soup!

There are a few different types of miso, but you'll usually find sweet, white miso (called shiro miso) in your supermarket, and it's a great addition to sauces, glazes, and even baked goods. Red or darker miso has a much bolder flavor and is best used in hearty stews.

Try my Maple Miso–Glazed Sweet Potatoes (page 199). They are a favorite!

SAVORY FLAVOR COMBINATIONS

Try these tasty tried-and-true combinations for rich, savory flavor.

- Miso + greens (try a kale and miso-butter sauté)
- Smoked paprika + chickpeas, gigantes, or butter beans (make Pan-Seared Beans and Greens, page 201)
- Seared mushrooms + garlic
- Roasted broccoli + Parmesan
- Popcorn + chili powder + nutritional yeast

PLANT LOVE COOKING

Preparing meal builders ahead of time and batch cooking makes it easier to create delicious plant-forward dishes throughout the week. This is a key approach to moving toward a plant-forward plate: The less time and effort you need to put in, the easier it is to shift your mindset and make this way of eating a habit, rather than a chore.

Preparation might sound like a lot of work, but it's easy! And once you get in the routine of having these building blocks at the ready, it will be easier to cook breakfast, lunch, and dinner throughout the week.

In the next few pages, I've made it easier for you by providing quick reference guides for roasting vegetables, cooking perfect grains, and cooking beans, peas, and lentils both on the stovetop and using an electric pressure cooker or slow cooker.

SET YOURSELF UP FOR SUCCESS

A few steps can help establish a routine to successfully get more plants on the table for easy and tasty meals.

1. **Take an inventory.** Go through your pantry, refrigerator, and freezer to see what you have and what's missing. Make a list of any missing ingredients for the recipes you want to make in the week ahead.

2. **Stock or restock the basics.** Make sure you have plenty of fruits and vegetables (fresh, frozen, and/or canned) on hand so that you can make quick and easy meals on demand. Buy only what you can reasonably eat before it goes bad.

3. **Choose foods and preparation methods that suit your lifestyle.** If you are usually short on time, plan to use quick-cooking red lentils on a busy weeknight and leave the longer-cooking beans and peas for the weekends. If you have the budget in exchange for time, buy precut or frozen fruits and vegetables that can easily be tossed into soups, stews, pastas, or smoothies.

4. **Chop (and clean) once, eat many times.** Next time you chop an onion, bell pepper, celery, or carrot for a recipe, chop what you need for the recipe—and maybe even more. Store any extra in the refrigerator or freezer to effortlessly add your favorite aromatics to your next recipe. This also makes it easy to whip up a quick omelet, soup, or stir-fry.

5. **Store your food properly.** Use the first-in, first-out method. To do this, simply arrange older foods in front or on top so you use them first. This works great for nonperishable items like canned beans or grains in the pantry and for foods like yogurt in the refrigerator. Reduce freezer burn by placing frozen fruits, vegetables, grains, and fish or meat in airtight, freezer-safe containers to help maintain their flavor, texture, and shelf life. Treat leafy fresh herbs like cut flowers: Put the cut end in an inch or two of water in a jar and store on a windowsill or in the refrigerator.

6. **Wait to wash most produce.** Water can hasten spoilage. Use a salad spinner or clean, lint-free kitchen towels to keep prepared greens dry. And when it comes to fresh berries, those are best rinsed just before you eat them.

7. **Use your freezer.** Store leftover soups, stews, chilis, pastas, muffins, and other baked goods in the freezer for a quick and easy meal later.

GUIDE TO ROASTING VEGETABLES

Roasting is one of the easiest ways to cook up *flavorful* vegetables with little effort and without a set recipe. Almost any vegetable (and many fruits) can be roasted, requiring just a few key steps to turn out a perfect pan of caramelized goodness.

Mind the cut. Cut vegetables into pieces of about the same size to ensure even cooking.

Use plenty of oil. Usually this is 1 or 2 tablespoons per pan. Though you don't want to saturate the vegetables, you do want to make sure each piece is coated. This helps the vegetables cook evenly and get crisp in the oven.

Make sure your oil tastes good. You might use avocado or olive oil, or give other more flavorful ones a try, such as toasted sesame, coconut, or walnut oil. But remember to store them properly. Oils left at room temperature or stored in warm areas for too long can go rancid and add off-flavors to your dish.

Season well. Salt is essential for bringing out the flavor of your vegetables. You can also add cracked black pepper, garlic or onion powder, dried herbs, smoked paprika, and other seasonings to the mix. Some vegetables—like white potatoes—can take more seasoning than others.

Tip: While hardy herbs like rosemary can stand the heat, if you're using fresh herbs such as parsley or dill, add those just before plating so that they don't burn in the hot oven.

Don't crowd the pan. Leaving space around the vegetables allows the hot air to come in close to roast each piece, leaving the edges well caramelized. Placing the vegetables too close together makes them steam and never get crispy. Use two baking sheets or cook the vegetables in batches if needed.

Use a hot oven. A properly heated oven is the key to even cooking. Preheat the oven to 425°F—give or take 25°.

Use convection if you have the option. This will speed up the cooking process and ensure an even air circulation. (Note: You can achieve the same or similar results using an air fryer, often in less time than it would take in a conventional oven.)

Below are general cooking times for various vegetables using a 425°F oven. You should turn the vegetables once, about midway through cooking.

Please note that the size you cut the vegetables will make a big difference in cooking time. The smaller the cut, the shorter the cook time. By example, roasting a halved winter squash takes 45 to 60 minutes while cubed squash takes 20 to 25 minutes. Similarly, turning down the heat for a slow roast requires more time.

Vegetables	Time at 425°F
Root vegetables (beets, carrots, whole garlic, onions, potatoes)	30 to 45 minutes
Winter squash (acorn, butternut, delicata)	20 to 25 minutes cubed; 45 to 60 minutes halved
Cabbages (broccoli, brussels sprouts, cauliflower florets)	15 to 25 minutes
Soft vegetables (bell peppers, summer squash, tomatoes)	15 to 20 minutes
Pencil-thin vegetables (asparagus, green beans)	10 to 20 minutes

This is a general guide to get you started. Remember that oven temperatures vary. When trying a new vegetable or roasting for the first time, be sure to check your veggies at the earliest time in the range to make sure they don't burn. Continue to check every few minutes until they are done—the edges should be a deep golden brown and there will be a rich aroma. Poke with a fork. For most vegetables, you'll know they are done and not overcooked when the fork meets a little resistance but doesn't slide all the way through.

ADD-ONS
These tasty additions to roasted vegetables will amp up their flavors even more.

Fresh herbs: Sprinkle fresh basil, cilantro, tarragon, parsley, or other herbs over the vegetables once they are cooked and ready to serve.

Parmesan or other cheese: Sprinkle over the vegetables at the halfway mark when turning them.

Citrus juice or vinegar: Squeeze or splash these on just before serving.

Vinaigrettes or dressings: Drizzle on just before serving or use as a dipping sauce on the side.

GUIDE TO ROASTING FRUIT

Many of the same rules of roasting apply when using fruit. But because fruit has a higher sugar content and tends to break down quicker, the cook times and temperatures are typically lower. To avoid a sticky mess, you might want to roast your fruit on a baking sheet lined with a silicone baking mat or parchment paper.

Fruits	Temperature and Time
Apples and pears, halved	350°F for 20 to 30 minutes
Berries (strawberries, grapes), whole	350°F for 20 minutes
Citrus (grapefruit, oranges), halved	Broil for 2 to 3 minutes
Stone fruit (nectarines, peaches, plums), halved	Broil for 5 to 7 minutes

GET GOING WITH GRAINS

Grains are an integral part of plant-based meals. Whole grains provide fiber and plant protein to help keep you feeling full and satisfied. They are also high in B vitamins for energy and a good source of minerals, such as magnesium, that help control blood pressure and regulate many processes in the body. Eating fiber-rich foods like whole grains has also been linked to a number of potential health benefits, including a lower risk for heart disease and stroke. The U.S. Department of Agriculture and U.S. Department of Health and Human Services' *Dietary Guidelines for Americans* recommends that at least half our grains be whole grains. Foods like oats, bulgur, brown rice, whole wheat, sorghum and even popcorn are easy picks. And though technically seeds, pseudo-grains like quinoa, amaranth, and buckwheat also count.

Pair cooked grains with stews to complete a meal, or use them as the base for a variety of dishes, including my Lentil-Stuffed Peppers (page 185), Red Rice (page 173), or Savory Quinoa Breakfast Bowls (page 85). You can also use them in a make-ahead mason-jar salad or as a simple side dressed with herbs and a homemade vinaigrette.

Choose your grain or pseudo-grain. Choose a grain that will best suit your taste buds and the recipe's needs. For example, brown rice adds nuttiness and chew to grain bowls, while quinoa can be a perfect filler for crispy veggie patties. Think about whether the recipe will be served warm (grits), cold (black rice), or room temperature (farro).

Try something new. Pop sorghum and sprinkle it with salt and your favorite spices for a snack. Make snack bars or granola using amaranth, or swap in half buckwheat flour when making pancakes.

Consider your time and other resources. White rice cooks quicker than brown rice, but brown rice is ideal for hands-free, quick cooking in a pressure or rice cooker. Quinoa tends to cost more than rice and may be harder to find. Luckily, many grains can be swapped for one another with equally delicious results.

Add flavor. Toasting the grains in a dry skillet or adding a tablespoon of butter or oil to the pan before the cooking liquid can help infuse additional flavor into your grains.

Pour in the liquid. Water is good to use for cooking grains, especially if you don't know exactly how you're going to eat them—savory or sweet. But you can also cook grains in broth, apple cider or other fruit juice, white wine, dairy or plant milk (such as coconut milk), or other liquids to add different, more robust flavors.

Add seasoning. Adding salt to the cooking liquid is ideal for the best infusion. Other herbs, spices, and ingredients can be added before, during, or after cooking, depending on the recipe and desired final texture and flavor.

WHERE TO BUY YOUR GRAINS

- Most major supermarkets stock a variety of grains. Check the rice, grains, or cereal aisle, as well as bulk bins and natural foods aisles.
- The bulk bins are a great place to start if you are trying out a new grain. This allows you to get one cup or less to test at home, rather than investing in a large amount. Hopefully, it will be a keeper, and you can go back for more.
- Though there may be slight variations in quality, most of the time, brand names don't matter when it comes to grains. You can buy in confidence knowing that the store-brand or bulk-bin grains will provide the exact same nutrition and flavor as the name brands.
- Running low on time? Look for quick-cooking and precooked grains that can range in preparation from 90 seconds in the microwave to a 10-minute boil on the stovetop. You'll also find frozen rice, quinoa, and mixed grains available in the freezer section of most specialty and standard supermarkets.
- Looking for another time-saver? Plan to cook your grains in an electric pressure cooker or on the stovetop ahead of time. You can freeze cooked grains for easy meals for months to come.

Note: Though we eat them like grains, quinoa and amaranth are technically seeds! Other pseudo-grains include buckwheat, millet, teff, and wild rice.

Scientifically speaking, these foods are not grains; however, they are incredibly nutritious, often providing more calcium, fiber, and protein than standard whole grains. So enjoy your "grains" in any form!

GUIDE TO COOKING GRAINS

If you can cook rice, you can cook any grain your heart desires. The general process for cooking most grains is simple:

1. Bring the grain and liquid to a boil in an appropriately sized pot.
2. Simmer, covered, for a defined time until the grain is cooked to the desired tenderness.
3. Let sit for 5 to 10 minutes.
4. Fluff with a fork (in most cases) or stir with a spoon before serving.

For more flavor, sub out water and use a good-quality vegetable or chicken stock.

GRAIN-COOKING-TIME CHEAT SHEET: STOVETOP

Grain (1 Cup Dry)	Liquid	Simmer	Yield	Good for . . .
Amaranth	2 cups	15 to 20 minutes	2½ cups	Porridge, granola, baked goods, pilaf
Barley	3 cups	45 to 60 minutes	3½ cups	Soup, mushroom entrées
Buckwheat	2 cups	20 minutes	4 cups	Salad, soup, granola, hot cereal
Bulgur	2 cups	10 to 12 minutes	2½ cups	Salad, tabbouleh
Farro (unsoaked)	2½ cups	30 minutes	3 cups	Salad, grain bowls
Fonio	2 cups	1 minute, let sit covered 5 minutes	4 cups	Hot cereal, pilaf, with stew
Grits (not quick)	4 cups	20 minutes	4 cups	Hot cereal
Millet	2½ cups	25 to 35 minutes	4 cups	Granola, warm grain bowls, salads, hot cereal
Oats (instant)	2 cups	1 minute	2 cups	Hot cereal
Oats (old-fashioned)	2 cups	5 minutes	2 cups	Hot cereal, baked goods
Oats (steel-cut)	4 cups	30 minutes	3 cups	Hot cereal, grain bowls
Quinoa	2 cups	15 minutes	3 cups	Grain bowls, stir-fries, sautés, burgers, patties
Rice, Black	2 cups	30 to 35 minutes	1⅓ cups	Cold salad, grain bowls
Rice, Brown	2 cups	45 to 50 minutes	3 cups	Grain bowls, burgers
Rice, White	2 cups	25 to 30 minutes	3 cups	Pilaf, rice pudding, as a side
Rice, Wild	3 cups	45 to 55 minutes	3½ cups	Pilaf, grain bowls
Sorghum	4 cups	50 to 60 minutes	3 cups	Salad, soup, porridge
Teff	3 cups	20 minutes	2½ cups	Porridge, stew

GUIDE TO COOKING DRIED BEANS, PEAS, AND LENTILS

You'll use a lot of pulses (also known as legumes; these are great for fiber and protein) when living a plant-forward lifestyle. Though canned beans are fine, this chart can come in handy when preparing dried beans for several recipes in this book.

In general, ½ cup of dry pulses yields about 1 cup cooked.

Type of Pulse	Soak	Pulse-to-Water Ratio	Cook Time
Beans	Yes	1 cup per 2 cups	1 to 2 hours (longer for fava beans and other larger beans)
Chickpeas	Yes	1 cup per 3 cups	1½ to 2 hours
Split Peas	No	1 cup per 2 cups	35 to 40 minutes
Lentils	No	1 cup per 2½ cups	Black/brown/green lentils: 20 to 40 minutes Red Lentils: Up to 15 minutes

TIPS

- Always look through your beans, peas, and lentils for stones or debris. Rinse them with water before cooking.
- If soaking is recommended: Cover the beans with cool water in a bowl or pot. Soak for 8 hours or overnight. Drain and rinse the beans with cool running water.
- Low on time? Do a quick soak. Boil 1 cup of beans with 3 cups of water for 3 minutes. Let sit for 1 hour. Drain and rinse with cool running water.

SKIP THE STOVETOP

Use a slow cooker or an electric pressure cooker to prepare your dried beans from scratch with ease.

Electric pressure cookers can shave hours off the cooking time and often don't require you to soak the beans in advance.

Without soaking, you can cook adzuki beans and black-eyed peas in under 20 minutes; black beans, navy beans, and pinto beans in about 20 to 25 minutes; and chickpeas and soybeans in 35 to 40 minutes. Soaking shaves off at least 5 minutes in each case. Lentils cook in under 10 minutes.

Remember, beans and peas will expand significantly as they cook. Take care not to fill the inner pot beyond the fill line.

Slow cookers make the process for cooking dried beans a breeze. Slowly cooking dried beans guarantees tender beans that are full of flavor. And the process is mostly hands-off.

Use a 3.5-quart slow cooker for 1 pound of beans or less.

To do this: Simply add the clean beans to the slow cooker and cover them with water, about 2 inches above the beans. Add onions, garlic, bay leaf, and any desired aromatics and seasonings and cook on low for 6 to 8 hours—begin checking the beans at the 5-hour mark if you're using a new slow cooker or working with a bean you haven't cooked before.

Note: Quick-cooking lentils will cook in much less time and can often be done in 2½ to 3 hours on high.

Keep in mind that some machines and some beans will cook more quickly than others. So the first few times you try cooking your beans, be sure to check a little earlier than the stated cook time to prevent them from becoming mushy or overcooked.

GO-TO MEAL AND SNACK IDEAS

Maybe you're limiting takeout and the drive-through, but you'll still have times when you don't feel like cooking. Thankfully, if you've followed the steps above, your kitchen will be stocked with healthy convenience foods that make it easy to whip up a meal or snack in no time.

FIVE-MINUTE MEALS

Egg tacos: Scrambled eggs + salsa + avocado + soft tortilla

Black bean salad: Cooked black or pinto beans + pico de gallo + frozen corn + avocado

Vegetable omelet: Two eggs + leftover vegetables

Chickpea-pasta salad: Chickpea pasta + grape tomatoes + extra-virgin olive oil + garlic powder + Italian seasoning

White bean and pesto pizza: Naan or prepared flatbread + pesto (page 72) + cooked white beans + arugula + mozzarella cheese

Hummus bowl: Hummus + olives + tomatoes + baby spinach (or other salad greens) + extra-virgin olive oil + lemon juice

Beans and rice bowl: Cooked pinto beans + chili-lime seasoning + tomatoes + frozen or precooked rice

Note: It's OK to take the easy route sometimes. Many of these recipes come together quickly using canned beans. You are welcome to cook your own from dried, but canned beans are just as nutritious!

NO-COOK MEALS

Mediterranean tuna (or white bean) lettuce wraps: Lettuce cups + canned tuna (or white beans) + chopped peppers and onions + olives + lemon vinaigrette

Super salad: Baby salad greens + mandarin oranges + chickpeas + chopped almonds + balsamic vinaigrette

Greek yogurt bowl: Plain Greek yogurt + roasted vegetables + prepared pesto

Smashed Chickpea Salad Sandwich: See page 127

SNACKS

These snack ideas are balanced for both flavor and nutrition. Some are make-ahead and meal-prep-friendly, while others are easy to simply grab and go. Add a few to your shopping list this week and delight in having satisfying snacks on hand!

- Steamed edamame + chili crisp oil
- Apple dipped in warm nut butter
- Pear + cheddar cheese
- Guacamole + red bell pepper sticks + chips
- Hummus + cucumbers + pita
- Dates stuffed with nut butter
- Banana + peanut butter
- Greek yogurt + berries
- Cottage cheese + pesto + grape tomatoes
- Cherry tomatoes + mozzarella cheese
- Mango + chili pepper + cashews
- Olives + marinated feta
- Roasted chickpeas + orange wedges
- Black bean dip + plantain chips
- Marinated tempeh or tofu bites
- Popcorn
- Grapes
- Fresh berries
- Handful of nuts or seeds

Check out the "Simple Snacks" chapter (page 96) so you always have delicious bites at the ready.

DIY NUT BUTTER

Making nut butter at home gives you the opportunity to experience the aroma and flavor of freshly roasted and ground almonds, peanuts, cashews, pecans, and more! You can also experiment with different add-ins to make the blend all your own. Try adding maple syrup and cinnamon, honey and vanilla, or cocoa powder for a chocolaty spin.

The base recipe takes just minutes, and all you need are two cups of your favorite nut or seed, a pinch of salt, and a high-speed blender or food processor.

If you're lucky enough to have a pecan tree in your yard—as some of us do in the southern states—roasted pecan butter will become a treat you'll look forward to every year. But you can also just buy fresh nuts from the bulk bins in your grocery store.

Depending on the ingredients' freshness, homemade nut butters will keep for at least a month in the refrigerator.

PECAN BUTTER

TAKES: 15 minutes
MAKES: about 1¼ cups

Love Note

You don't have to use pecans. Go with your favorite nut, be it peanuts, walnuts, almonds, or cashews, or even sunflower or pumpkin seeds. Use the same amount as you would pecans.

Ingredients

- 2 cups raw pecan halves
- ½ teaspoon kosher salt
- 2 to 3 tablespoons maple syrup or honey (optional)
- ½ teaspoon ground cinnamon (optional)

Directions

1. Preheat the oven to 350°F.

2. Spread the pecans in a single layer on a sheet pan and roast in the oven for 5 minutes. Stir, then roast for an additional 3 to 5 minutes until they're nutty and slightly browned. Don't let the nuts burn.

3. Put the warm pecans in the bowl of a food processor or a high-powered blender. Pulse until the pecans are coarsely ground. Scrape down the sides of the bowl.

4. Process on high 1 to 2 minutes. Scrape down the sides. Process an additional 3 to 5 minutes or until smooth and creamy, scraping down the sides as needed.

5. Add the salt, and, if using, the maple syrup or honey and the cinnamon. Process just until incorporated.

Tips
- ✓ Roast or toast the nuts. Doing this helps provide more depth and flavor, as well as a creamier texture. Adjust the roasting time as needed—sunflower seeds and pecans will burn faster and blend to a butter faster than almonds, for example.
- ✓ Use a quality food processor or high-powered blender for the best results. Nuts, especially almonds, are hard and require a powerful motor to go from a nut paste to a smooth, creamy, drippy nut butter.

DIY FRUIT JAM

Making jam is easier than you think. Sure, canning jam can feel a little intimidating, but there are other options. You can make a refrigerator or freezer jam without the need for a water bath or the risk involved with ensuring a proper seal.

The recipe for fruit jam is simple. Cook fresh or frozen fruit with sugar, honey, or your favorite sweetener over low heat until the fruit releases its juices. Make it as simple or complex as you'd like when it comes to flavors.

My favorite trick: Use chia seeds to get that characteristic gel-like texture of a real jam within minutes.

STRAWBERRY CHIA JAM

TAKES: 10 minutes
MAKES: 1½ cups

Ingredients

- **2 cups fresh or frozen hulled strawberries**
- **1 tablespoon fresh lemon juice**
- **1 to 2 tablespoons honey (or maple syrup or granulated sugar if vegan)**
- **2 tablespoons chia seeds**

Directions

1. Cook the strawberries in a small saucepan over medium heat. Once the fruit starts to break down, use a potato masher or fork to mash it into smaller pieces. Continue to cook, stirring frequently, until the mixture becomes slightly syrupy and the fruit is cooked through.

2. Remove from the heat and stir in the lemon juice, honey (or other sweetener), and chia seeds. Stir until well combined. Let stand for at least 5 minutes, until the jam starts to thicken.

3. Serve at room temperature or let cool, then transfer to a jar with a lid and store in the refrigerator for up to 2 weeks. The jam will become thicker once chilled.

Love Note

Don't like the visible chia seeds peeking through? Try chia flour or white chia seeds. These are typically available at health food stores and specialty markets.

Tips
✓ Swap in the same amount of fresh or frozen blackberries, blueberries, or raspberries, or a mixture of a few types of berries, to make this jam.
✓ Adjust the amount of honey you use based on the sweetness of your berries and your personal preference.

Love Note

Repurpose
the strained pulp
in muffins
or oatmeal.

DIY PLANT MILK

It's incredibly easy to make plant milk at home. You just need a high-powered blender; filtered water; a nut milk bag or sieve and cheesecloth; and your nut, seed, or grain of choice. These easy-to-make milks can be kept on hand to use in coffee and tea lattes, cereal, sauces, and baked goods. Each makes about a quart of milk (4 cups). Homemade plant milk will last three to five days in a sealed jar in the refrigerator—a much shorter shelf life than those you buy in the store. Keep that in mind before blending a batch, and consider how much you'll actually need in the next few days.

To store extra plant milk—whether store-bought or homemade—freeze the excess in ice cube trays and store the cubes in a sealed, labeled, freezer-safe container for up to three months.

OAT MILK

TAKES: 5 minutes
MAKES: 4 cups

Ingredients

- 3 cups cool filtered water
- 1 cup old-fashioned oats
- 2 pitted dates
- 1 teaspoon vanilla extract (optional)
- Pinch of salt

Directions

1. Put all the ingredients in a high-powered blender and blend for about 30 seconds. Do not overblend.
2. Strain the oat milk with a sieve and cheesecloth or nut milk bag into a jar with a lid. Shake well before pouring into tea or coffee or over cereal.

NUT MILK

TAKES: 5 minutes (plus overnight soak)
MAKES: 4 cups

Ingredients

- 4 cups filtered water
- 1 cup almonds, cashews, pecans, or pistachios, soaked overnight and drained
- 2 tablespoons pure maple syrup (or 2 pitted dates)
- 1 teaspoon vanilla extract
- Pinch of coarse salt

Directions

1. Put all the ingredients in a high-powered blender. Blend on high 1 to 2 minutes or until smooth (time varies by blender).
2. Strain the nut milk with a sieve and cheesecloth or nut milk bag into a jar with a lid. Shake well before serving.

HEMP MILK

TAKES: 5 minutes
MAKES: 4 cups

Ingredients

- 4 cups cool filtered water
- ½ cup hemp hearts
- 2 pitted dates
- Pinch of salt

Directions

1. Put the water and hemp hearts in a high-powered blender and blend for about 30 seconds.
2. Pour the hemp milk into a jar using a funnel and sieve to strain out any large pieces. Shake before serving.

DIY SAVORY SAUCES

Sometimes a simple sauce is the key to taking a dish from basic to brilliant. The following recipes are a sample of what you can do to add extra flavor, color, and more nutrition to your meals.

Make each with what you have on hand and drizzle them on almost everything. These are all about the flavor!

PEANUT SAUCE

TAKES: 5 minutes
MAKES: about 1 cup

Ingredients

- ½ cup creamy natural peanut butter
- 1 tablespoon soy sauce (or coconut aminos)
- 2 tablespoons honey (or brown sugar if vegan)
- 2 tablespoons apple cider vinegar
- 1 teaspoon hot sauce
- ¼ teaspoon salt, or to taste
- ¼ to ⅓ cup hot water

Directions

Whisk the peanut butter, soy sauce, honey, apple cider vinegar, hot sauce, and salt in a small bowl. Add hot water to thin the sauce, 1 tablespoon at a time, until the sauce is smooth—slightly thinner than the consistency of honey. Enjoy right away or store in the refrigerator for up to a week.

Swaps:

- ✓ Swap in natural almond or cashew butter for the peanut butter.
- ✓ Use 1 tablespoon of tamari or coconut aminos in place of the soy sauce.
- ✓ Use equal amounts of maple syrup or brown sugar for the honey. If using brown sugar, dissolve it in the hot water before adding to the sauce for easier blending.
- ✓ Use equal amounts of rice vinegar or lime juice in place of the apple cider vinegar. (Using lime juice will reduce the shelf life.)
- ✓ Trade chili paste or sriracha for the hot sauce, or use crushed red chili flakes for heat.

LIME RANCH DRESSING

TAKES: 5 minutes
MAKES: about 1 cup

Ingredients

- ½ cup Greek yogurt (or vegan mayonnaise)
- ¼ cup chopped fresh cilantro
- 2 garlic cloves, peeled and grated
- ½ teaspoon onion powder
- ½ lime, juiced
- ½ teaspoon salt

Directions

Whisk all the ingredients in a small bowl or puree in a small blender. Enjoy right away or store refrigerated in a sealed jar for up to 3 days.

BLENDER SALSA

TAKES: 5 minutes
MAKES: 2½ cups

Ingredients

- 1 (28-ounce) can fire-roasted whole tomatoes, drained and liquid reserved (or 8 roasted fresh plum tomatoes)
- 1 medium onion (red, sweet, or white), roughly chopped
- 1 medium jalapeño, ribs and seeds removed
- ½ cup fresh cilantro, chopped
- 2 garlic cloves, peeled
- 1 lime, juiced
- ½ teaspoon salt
- 1 teaspoon sugar (optional)

Directions

1. Pulse the tomatoes, onion, jalapeño, cilantro, garlic, lime juice and salt in a food processor or blender until the mixture reaches the desired consistency. Add the reserved tomato liquid as needed to thin the salsa.

2. Taste for seasoning. Add sugar, if using, and additional salt as needed.

3. Serve chilled or at room temperature, or store in an airtight container for up to 3 days.

 Tips

- ✓ Drain the canned tomatoes over a bowl to catch the liquid.
- ✓ Roast the onion and whole jalapeño pepper in the oven for an added flavor dimension.
- ✓ Leave the ribs in the jalapeño for a hotter salsa.

CHIPOTLE MAYO

Takes: 5 minutes
Makes: about 1 cup

Ingredients

- ½ cup mayonnaise (or vegan mayonnaise)
- 1 chipotle in adobo sauce
- ½ tablespoon adobo sauce
- 1 garlic clove, peeled
- ½ lime, juiced
- Salt, to taste

Directions

Put all the ingredients in a small blender. Puree until smooth and well combined. Enjoy right away or store refrigerated in a sealed jar for up to 3 days.

 Tip

- ✓ You can typically find 7-ounce cans of chipotles in adobo in the canned vegetable or international foods aisle at most major supermarkets.

DIY PESTO

Pestos are a quick and easy way to add a boost of flavor and vegetables to a variety of dishes. Make a batch to toss with pasta or to marinate cooked chickpeas or cannellini beans. Pestos can also be served as a dip, whisked into vinaigrettes, or drizzled over roasted vegetables and scrambled eggs.

Here are two pesto recipes to get you started, but feel free to play around with variations once you've mastered the basics. Next, you might try a basil-pistachio pesto, a red pepper–almond pesto, or an arugula-walnut version.

KALE WALNUT PESTO

TAKES: 5 minutes
MAKES: 1 cup

Ingredients

- 4 cups (packed) baby kale
- ⅓ cup toasted walnuts
- 3 garlic cloves, peeled
- ¼ cup Parmesan cheese
- ½ to 1 teaspoon coarse salt (adjust to taste based on the Parmesan's saltiness)
- ½ cup high-quality extra-virgin olive oil

Directions

Pulse the kale, walnuts, garlic, Parmesan, and salt in a food processor until well chopped. With the food processor running on low, add the olive oil until well blended and smooth. Store leftovers in an airtight jar for up to a week, or freeze in an ice cube tray and store in a freezer-safe container for up to 6 months.

VEGAN PESTO

TAKES: 5 minutes
MAKES: ½ cup

Ingredients

- ½ cup toasted walnuts
- 2 cups (packed) baby spinach or baby kale
- 2 tablespoons nutritional yeast
- 1 tablespoon fresh lemon juice
- 2 garlic cloves, peeled
- Coarse salt, to taste
- Crushed red pepper flakes (optional)
- ½ cup high-quality extra-virgin olive oil

Directions

Put the toasted walnuts, spinach or kale, nutritional yeast, lemon juice, garlic, salt, and crushed red pepper flakes, if using, in a small blender or food processor. Pulse until chopped. Using the puree setting, with the blades running, stream the olive oil into the mixture. Puree until thoroughly blended. Store leftovers in an airtight jar for up to a week, or freeze in an ice cube tray and store in a freezer-safe container for up to 6 months.

 Tip ✓ Parmesan cheese provides depth of flavor and is a key ingredient in traditional pesto. When you're making a vegan pesto, nutritional yeast helps impart a similar umami flavor.

Love Note

Try different variations:
Swap in basil, arugula,
or other greens for
the spinach
or kale.

DIY VINAIGRETTES

Once you see how easy it is to make homemade salad dressing, you'll probably stop reaching for the bottled ones!

Homemade vinaigrettes taste fresher and, depending on the ingredients, can last up to two weeks in the refrigerator. You can use any jar with a lid, a whisk and a bowl, or a blender to pull these together.

A standard vinaigrette usually follows the same ratio: three parts oil to one part acid (such as vinegar or citrus juice).

Dressings made simply with vinegar, oil, salt, and pepper will last up to two weeks in the refrigerator. Adding garlic, shallots, and citrus juice or other more perishable ingredients will reduce the shelf life.

Consider using different types of oils and acids. Pick one of each and shake.

Recommended oils: Extra-virgin olive, toasted sesame, peanut, walnut, and roasted pumpkin seed oil

Recommended acids: Citrus juices (including lime, orange, lemon, grapefruit, and tangerine juice) and vinegars (including champagne, red wine, balsamic, apple cider, black, rice, or sherry vinegar)

LEMON VINAIGRETTE

TAKES: 5 minutes
MAKES: 1 cup

Ingredients

- ⅔ cup extra-virgin olive oil
- ⅓ cup freshly squeezed lemon juice
- Salt, to taste
- Freshly ground black pepper, to taste
- 1 tablespoon honey or brown sugar (optional)
- Minced garlic or shallots (optional)
- Chopped fresh parsley (optional)

Directions

Put all the ingredients in a jar. Shake until combined. Enjoy right away or seal and store in the refrigerator for up to 3 days.

BASIC BALSAMIC VINAIGRETTE

TAKES: 5 minutes
MAKES: 1 cup

Ingredients

- ¾ cup extra-virgin olive oil
- ¼ cup good-quality balsamic vinegar
- Salt, to taste
- Freshly ground black pepper, to taste
- 1 teaspoon Dijon mustard (optional)
- 1 tablespoon honey or brown sugar (optional)

Directions

Put all the ingredients in a jar. Shake until combined. Enjoy right away or seal and store in the refrigerator for up to 3 days.

 Tip   ✓ For variations, add small amounts of minced fresh herbs, garlic, or shallots.

DIY SPICE MIXES

The key to any tasty dish is good flavor—and that can come from the spices you're using. Rather than buying blends off the store shelf, consider making your own spice mixtures to liven up dishes.

TACO SEASONING

Takes: 5 minutes
Makes: about 3 tablespoons

Ingredients

- 1 tablespoon chili powder (plain, not chipotle)
- 1 teaspoon cumin
- ¾ teaspoon kosher salt
- 1 teaspoon garlic powder
- 1 teaspoon onion powder
- 1 teaspoon smoked paprika
- 1 teaspoon oregano

Directions

1. Combine all ingredients in a small jar with a lid. Shake until evenly mixed.
2. Store in an airtight container in a cool, dry place.

BBQ SEASONING

Takes: 5 minutes
Makes: about 3 tablespoons

Ingredients

- 1 tablespoon brown sugar
- 1 tablespoon smoked paprika
- 1 teaspoon garlic powder
- 1 teaspoon onion powder
- 1 teaspoon kosher salt
- ½ teaspoon freshly ground black pepper
- ½ teaspoon dry mustard

Directions

1. Combine all ingredients in a small jar with a lid. Shake until evenly mixed.
2. Store in an airtight container in a cool, dry place.

 Tips
- ✓ It's important to use fresh spices for the best flavor.
- ✓ Add 1 teaspoon cornstarch as an anti-clumping agent and to help thicken dishes.

The Recipes

Part 2

BREAKFAST

BAKED EGGS AND GREENS

PREP: 15 minutes
COOK: 35 minutes
SERVES: 4

Inspired by North African shakshuka—and a desire to eat more veggies in the morning—these spiced, baked green eggs are perfect for breakfast, lunch, or dinner. This recipe swaps in kale for a green spin on the traditional tomato and red bell pepper sauce. It's a hearty dish that's suitable for a weekday and yet elegant enough for a special occasion.

Love Note

Kale is a plant-based source of calcium, which is important in maintaining bone strength.

Ingredients

- ¼ cup extra-virgin olive oil
- 1 small sweet onion, diced
- 3 garlic cloves, peeled and minced
- 1 teaspoon ground coriander
- ¼ teaspoon red pepper flakes (more if you like heat)
- 6 cups thinly sliced kale
- ½ cup vegetable stock or water

- 4 large eggs
- Coarse salt
- Freshly cracked black pepper
- ½ cup crumbled feta (about 2 ounces)
- ¼ cup chopped sun-dried tomatoes
- Hot sauce, for topping
- Fresh herbs, for topping
- Crusty bread, for serving

Directions

1. Preheat the oven to 350°F.

2. Heat the olive oil in a 10-inch oven-safe skillet over medium-low heat. Sauté the onion until softened, about 7 to 8 minutes.

3. Add the garlic, coriander, and red pepper flakes. Cook about 1 minute.

4. Add the kale and sauté for about 3 minutes, taking care to combine all ingredients well.

5. Add the stock or water. Cover and cook for 7 to 10 minutes, or until the kale is tender and most of the liquid is absorbed.

6. Use the back of a spoon to create 4 wells in the greens. Carefully crack an egg into each well.

7. Sprinkle the greens and eggs with salt and black pepper, to taste, and top with the feta and sun-dried tomatoes.

8. Transfer to the preheated oven. Bake until the whites of the eggs are set, about 10 to 12 minutes. Top with hot sauce and herbs, and serve warm with bread.

Tip ✓ Take care not to overcook the greens. The cook time works for thinly sliced kale, but adjust the cooking time to accommodate the greens you have on hand. Cook spinach for a much shorter time than kale or collard greens, for example.

MAKE-AHEAD SPINACH BREAKFAST WRAPS

PREP: 15 minutes
COOK: 30 minutes
MAKES: 8 wraps

I love to stash an extra breakfast dish in the freezer for busy weekday mornings. If you haven't tried this strategy, just know that having one less thing to decide on a busy day is a gift to your future self. These hearty breakfast wraps will power you through the morning and are so easy to make. With only 15 minutes of hands-on prep, these freezer-friendly wraps will be your new favorite grab-and-go breakfast.

Ingredients

- 4 ounces cream cheese (or vegan cream cheese), at room temperature
- ½ cup chopped, drained, oil-packed sun-dried tomatoes
- ½ teaspoon garlic powder
- Black pepper, to taste
- 2 tablespoons olive oil, divided
- 1 pound baby spinach
- Salt, to taste
- 8 large eggs
- 8 soft tortillas (white corn, whole-grain, or grain-free), lightly warmed until pliable

Directions

1. In a small bowl, stir the cream cheese, sun-dried tomatoes, garlic powder, and pepper until combined.

2. Heat 1 tablespoon of the olive oil in a large skillet over medium heat. Add the spinach and cook, stirring occasionally, until wilted, about 5 minutes. Season with salt and pepper. Squeeze the spinach in a clean kitchen towel or paper towel to remove excess liquid. Do not skip this step.

3. Whisk the eggs and 1 tablespoon of water in a large bowl until the yolks and whites are blended. Wipe the skillet clean. Heat the remaining 1 tablespoon of olive oil over medium-low heat. Add the whisked eggs to the heated skillet, and season with salt and pepper to taste. Cook until the eggs are set, about 3 minutes.

4. Assemble the wraps. Spread 1 tablespoon of the cream cheese mixture onto each tortilla, then layer ⅛ of the spinach and ⅛ of the eggs. Roll up the tortilla (folding the sides in then rolling up from the bottom and tucking tightly) and return it to the warm skillet, seam side down, to toast. Cut in half if desired and serve immediately, or let cool to freeze.

To freeze: Let the wraps cool completely in a single layer on a parchment paper–lined baking sheet, seam side down. Add to a freezer-safe container and store for up to 3 months.

To reheat: Place the wraps in a conventional or toaster oven, seam side down, and bake until heated through, about 12 to 15 minutes.

Make it vegan: Scramble a plant-based egg equivalent according to package directions as a swap for the 8 eggs. And swap vegan cream cheese for regular.

Tips

- ✓ Most burrito- or fajita-size tortillas will work. Avoid corn tortillas for this recipe, since they are more prone to cracking and may not fare as well in the freezer.
- ✓ Don't have spinach? Use your favorite greens: Baby kale, arugula, or a blend of baby greens will work.

CHICKPEA BREAKFAST SCRAMBLE

PREP: 10 minutes
COOK: 5 minutes
SERVES: 2

A question I often get from vegetarians and those transitioning to a more plant-forward way of eating is how to get more protein at breakfast without eggs. Though chia seed pudding and tofu scrambles are great options, this savory scramble made with chickpea flour is a solid choice as well. Chickpeas are packed with protein and fiber—plus this recipe can be made in about the same time it takes to scramble an egg.

Ingredients

- ½ cup chickpea flour
- ½ cup vegetable broth
- ½ teaspoon onion powder
- ¼ teaspoon turmeric
- ¼ teaspoon salt
- ⅛ teaspoon black pepper
- 1 tablespoon olive oil or butter
- Hot sauce, for topping
- Chives, for topping
- Sautéed vegetables, for topping

Directions

1. In a medium bowl, whisk the chickpea flour, broth, onion powder, turmeric, salt, and pepper until smooth. Let the batter sit for 10 minutes until the flour is fully hydrated.

2. Heat the oil or butter in a nonstick skillet over medium heat. Add the batter. Cook undisturbed for about 1 minute, until the batter begins to firm on the bottom. Take care to not let it get too brown.

3. Using a nonstick spatula, move the batter around in large curds until it reaches a scrambled appearance and all the batter is firm with no wet spots remaining.

4. Top with hot sauce, chives, and sautéed vegetables, and serve with roasted potatoes, toast, and/or walnut breakfast patties (page 86).

Love Note

Turmeric delivers brilliant color to many popular recipes and is a source of curcumin, a strong antioxidant with impressive anti-inflammatory properties.

Tips

✓ Can't find chickpea flour? Blend your own. Simply grind dried (uncooked) chickpeas in a blender until they become a fine powder.
✓ For an "eggy" flavor, you can use black salt (*kala namak*), but it can be pricey and difficult to find.
✓ Sauté peppers, onions, mushrooms, or tomatoes in the skillet before scrambling your chickpea batter for a veggie-rich breakfast.

SAVORY QUINOA BREAKFAST BOWLS

PREP: 5 minutes
COOK: 15 minutes
SERVES: 2

I love a savory breakfast. In fact, the first time I ever had quinoa was for breakfast. Now I like to prepare a big pot of quinoa to use for salads, sides, and bowls just like this one. Using it as a base is the perfect way to add in some extra fiber and protein to your meal, while also getting a jump start on your vegetables for the day. This bowl is balanced with hearty mushrooms, tasty tomatoes, plenty of greens, and creamy avocado to finish it off.

Love Note

With all nine essential amino acids, quinoa is a complete source of protein and an excellent source of fiber.

Ingredients

- 2 tablespoons olive oil
- 2 cups sliced fresh mushrooms such as shiitake or baby bella
- 1 cup grape tomatoes, whole
- 2 garlic cloves, peeled and minced or pressed
- 2 eggs
- Salt, to taste
- Black pepper, to taste
- 1 cup cooked quinoa
- 2 cups arugula, baby spinach, or baby kale
- 1 avocado, sliced

Directions

1. Heat the olive oil in a large skillet over medium heat. Add the mushrooms, grape tomatoes, and garlic. Sauté for about 5 to 7 minutes, until the tomatoes burst and the mushrooms start to caramelize.

2. Push the vegetables to the side and crack the eggs in the skillet. Season with salt and pepper to taste. Cook for 1 to 2 minutes per side, until the whites and yolks are firm.

3. Assemble the bowls: Place ½ cup of the quinoa in the bottom of a bowl. Top with ½ cup of the greens, 1 cooked egg, and ½ the tomato and mushroom mixture. Repeat for the second bowl. Top both with sliced avocado and pepper to taste.

Make-ahead vegetable preparation: Toss the mushrooms and tomatoes with 2 tablespoons olive oil, 2 minced garlic cloves, and salt and pepper to taste. Roast in the oven at 400°F for 20 minutes. Store in the refrigerator for up to 3 days. Reheat in the skillet before cooking the eggs.

Make-ahead quinoa: Rinse 1 cup quinoa under cool running water. Drain. Toast the quinoa over medium heat in a saucepan to evaporate any excess water. Add 1¾ cups water or broth and bring to a boil. Reduce the heat to low and simmer, covered, for 15 minutes. Remove from the heat and let stand, covered, for 15 minutes. Fluff and eat, or cool and refrigerate for up to 5 days, or freeze for up to 2 to 3 months until you're ready to make these bowls.

Tips

✓ If using a plant-based egg alternative, prepare according to package directions in the skillet with the vegetables.
✓ Don't have quinoa? Swap in cooked rice or barley.

WALNUT BREAKFAST PATTIES

PREP: 5 minutes
COOK: 12 minutes
MAKES: 8 patties

Truth be told, I'm not a big fan of foods pretending to be other foods. But with meaty walnuts, sage, cayenne, garlic, and a little sweetness from maple syrup, these patties do taste a lot like sausage. I love making them to serve with grits, on top of a breakfast salad, or to simply eat with a waffle. Packed with good fats, fiber, and lots of flavor, these patties are a delicious and easy way to enjoy a meat substitute with benefits.

Ingredients

- 1½ cups walnuts
- ½ cup old-fashioned oats
- 1 large egg
- 1 tablespoon maple syrup
- 1 teaspoon rubbed sage
- 1 teaspoon garlic powder
- ¾ teaspoon salt
- ¼ teaspoon cayenne pepper
- Avocado oil, olive oil, or other neutral oil, for frying

Directions

1. Pulse all the ingredients except the oil in a food processor until the walnuts and oats are well moistened and a soft ball starts to form. The dough will be sticky.

2. Using wet hands, form the dough into 8 patties.

3. Heat 2 or 3 tablespoons of oil in a medium skillet over medium-high heat. Lower the patties in batches into the oil. Cook about 4 minutes per side, until golden on each side. Remove and let rest on a paper towel–lined plate or cooling rack to allow any excess oil to drip off.

4. Serve warm.

Love Note

Research suggests that eating walnuts may be connected to improved brain and heart health.

 Tip   ✓ Check your walnuts before starting. Walnuts are high in polyunsaturated fats that can go bad over time, leaving a bitter aftertaste. Store your walnuts in the freezer or refrigerator for longer shelf life and the best flavor.

NUTTY CARAMELIZED BANANA AND STEEL-CUT OATS

PREP: 5 minutes
COOK: 30 minutes
SERVES: 4

Most mornings, I'm the kind of cook to simply toss oats in the microwave while getting dressed. But every now and then, it's fun to get fancy with oats. Enter buttery caramelized bananas drizzled with warm, drippy peanut butter. This is a satisfying and fun breakfast. Steel-cut oats take longer to cook than other oats, but the irresistible chewy, nutty flavor they deliver is definitely worth the wait.

Ingredients

- 3 tablespoons butter (or vegan butter), divided
- 1 cup steel-cut oats
- 4 cups water (or milk)
- ⅛ teaspoon salt
- 2 small bananas, peeled and sliced long or into ¾-inch-thick rounds
- ¼ cup natural peanut butter, or more to taste, warmed
- Crushed peanuts (optional)

Directions

1. **Cook the oats.** Heat 1 tablespoon of the butter in a 2-quart saucepan over medium heat. Add the oats and make sure they are well coated in the butter. Stir frequently until the oats smell fragrant and nutty, about 3 minutes. Carefully add the water and salt.

2. Let the water come to a boil. Reduce the heat to low and simmer, covered, for 20 to 30 minutes. Stir occasionally, taking care to scrape the bottom of the pan. When done, the oats will be tender and creamy.

3. **Caramelize the bananas.** Heat the remaining 2 tablespoons of butter in a medium skillet over medium heat. Add the banana slices. If needed, cook in batches to avoid crowding the skillet. Cook undisturbed for about 2 minutes. (The bananas will release easily when caramelized.) Flip using tongs and cook for about 1 minute on the other side.

4. **Assemble the bowls.** Portion the cooked oats evenly into 4 bowls. Top evenly with bananas, drizzle with warm peanut butter, and sprinkle with chopped peanuts, if desired. Serve warm.

Tips

- ✓ Use 4 cups of your favorite milk instead of water (or a mix of both) for a creamier texture.
- ✓ To warm peanut butter, heat it in a small saucepan on the stovetop over low heat, or microwave it in a microwave-safe bowl for 30 seconds or until it melts to the consistency of honey.
- ✓ You can cook the oats ahead of time and keep them refrigerated in a sealed container for up to 5 days. To reheat: Add a splash of water or milk and warm in the microwave, covered, for 1 minute, or in a small pot on the stovetop until heated through.
- ✓ Use natural peanut or almond butter. Look for the kind that needs to be stirred and is runny at room temperature. If you can't find that, you might need to slightly heat the nut butter to loosen it up.
- ✓ Need a little more sweetness? Top with maple syrup or brown sugar.

CARAMELIZED PEARS WITH WALNUTS AND YOGURT

PREP: 10 minutes
COOK: 30 minutes
SERVES: 4

These sweet, caramelized pears are proof that a hot oven can transform a simple piece of fruit into an elegant creation. Pears are often overlooked in favor of apples, but I look forward to enjoying fresh Anjou, Bosc, and especially Comice (or Christmas pears) every fall. I like to serve these caramelized pears for a holiday brunch with friends or family or as a simple Sunday breakfast. Topped with creamy yogurt and toasted walnuts for crunch and a dose of omega-3s, this is a complete meal.

Ingredients

- ¼ cup maple syrup
- ½ teaspoon ground cinnamon
- ½ teaspoon vanilla extract
- Pinch of kosher salt
- 4 ripe but firm pears such as Bartlett, Bosc, Anjou, or Concorde
- 1 cup Greek yogurt (or vegan yogurt)
- ½ cup chopped walnuts, toasted
- Fresh thyme leaves, for garnish

Directions

1. Preheat the oven to 400°F. Line a large sheet pan with parchment paper.

2. In a small bowl, stir the maple syrup, cinnamon, vanilla extract, and salt until smooth. Set the glaze aside.

3. Keeping the skin on, slice the pears in half. Scoop out the seeds. Slice a sliver off the round bottom of each half so they lay flat. Place the pears on the sheet pan about 2 inches apart, cut side up. Spoon or brush half the glaze evenly over the pears.

4. Turn the pears cut side down on the pan. Roast for 15 to 20 minutes, until the pears begin to caramelize to a deep golden brown—taking care not to burn the glaze. Flip the pears and finish roasting, about 5 to 10 minutes more, until they are easily pierced with a fork but not too soft.

5. Dollop each pear half with ¼ cup of the yogurt. Drizzle with the reserved glaze and sprinkle with walnuts and fresh thyme (if using). Serve.

 Tip ✓ This recipe tastes best when pears are in season, during cool-weather months.

PEACH ALMOND BAKED OATMEAL

PREP: 10 minutes
COOK: 30 minutes
SERVES: 8

Slightly reminiscent of a summer peach cobbler, this baked oatmeal is one of my favorite ways to feed a crowd. The smell of bubbling brown sugar, cinnamon, and peaches will call everyone to the breakfast table. Maximize flavor and sweetness with fresh, juicy end-of-season peaches, or use frozen peaches any time of the year. This forgiving recipe can be made vegan with a few swaps. Serve topped with yogurt, honey, and toasted almonds for extra flavor and flair.

Ingredients

- 2 cups old-fashioned oats
- 1½ cups milk of choice
- 1 egg, beaten (or 2 tablespoons flaxseed meal)
- 1 tablespoon butter (or vegan butter), melted
- ¼ to ½ cup brown sugar, coconut sugar, or maple syrup (based on sweetness preference)
- ¼ cup sliced almonds
- 1 teaspoon vanilla extract
- 1 teaspoon ground cinnamon
- ¼ teaspoon ground nutmeg
- Pinch of salt
- 2 ripe peaches, thinly sliced (about 1½ cups)
- Greek or vegan yogurt, for serving (optional)

Directions

1. Preheat the oven to 375°F.

2. In a medium bowl, stir all the ingredients except the peaches and yogurt until well combined.

3. Spray an 8-by-8-inch baking dish with cooking spray. Pour the oat mixture into the dish. Top it with the peaches. Bake for 25 to 30 minutes, or until the edges are bubbly and slightly browned.

4. Serve warm. Top with additional peaches, almonds, maple syrup, or yogurt, if desired.

5. Store leftovers covered in the refrigerator for up to 4 days.

Make it vegan: Use plant milk and vegan butter. Substitute 2 tablespoons of ground flaxseed for the egg.

Tips
- ✓ Taste your peaches and adjust the sugar according to your sweetness preference.
- ✓ Fresh ripe or overripe summer peaches offer the best flavor. But use canned peaches (drained) or thawed frozen peaches if that's what you have available.
- ✓ If you're not into the fuzzy fruit, swap the peaches for plums or even cherries.

BLUEBERRY BUTTERMILK OAT MUFFINS

PREP: 20 minutes
COOK: 20 minutes
MAKES: 1 dozen muffins

Wake up with the aroma of fresh blueberry muffins, and feel good knowing that these have a healthyish slant! Bursting with sweet blueberry flavor and balanced with buttermilk, these lightly sweetened muffins are guaranteed to be a new family favorite. I love making a double batch—one to enjoy fresh for breakfast with a side of yogurt or as a snack, and one to freeze for another day. Believe me, you'll want to keep these on hand at all times.

Love Note

Nourish your heart!
The polyphenols
in blueberries have been
shown to help decrease
blood pressure–a key factor
in heart disease.

Ingredients

- 1 cup uncooked old-fashioned oats
- 1 cup buttermilk
- 1 cup all-purpose flour
- 1 teaspoon baking powder
- ½ teaspoon baking soda
- ½ teaspoon salt
- ½ cup sugar
- 1 egg, beaten
- ¼ cup butter (or vegan butter), melted, or neutral oil
- 1 teaspoon vanilla extract
- 1½ cups fresh blueberries

CRUNCHY TOPPING:
(optional but recommended)
- 2 tablespoons brown sugar
- 2 tablespoons butter (or vegan butter), melted

Directions

1. Place a rack in the middle position of the oven and preheat the oven to 400°F. Spray a standard 12-well muffin tin with oil or use muffin-tin liners.

2. In a large bowl, combine the oats and buttermilk. Soak for 15 minutes.

3. In a second bowl, whisk the flour, baking powder, baking soda, and salt.

4. Stir the sugar, egg, butter or oil, and vanilla extract into the oat-buttermilk mixture. Then add the dry ingredients. Stir until just combined, being careful not to overmix. Gently fold the blueberries into the batter.

5. If using the crunchy topping, stir the brown sugar and butter together until the sugar dissolves.

6. Spoon the batter into the prepared muffin tin. If using the crunchy topping, spoon it evenly over the muffin batter.

7. Bake for 15 to 18 minutes, until a toothpick inserted into the center of one or two muffins comes out clean.

8. Let the muffins cool in the pan for 5 minutes, then transfer them to a cooling rack.

Tips

✓ Frozen blueberries are just as healthy as fresh ones and work perfectly in this recipe. Simply thaw and drain the berries before adding them to the muffin batter.
✓ Want a dairy-free muffin? Substitute 1 cup of plant milk for the buttermilk. The flavor will change, and the muffins will lose some tenderness, but they'll still taste great.
✓ To freeze and reheat: Let the muffins cool, then place them in a single layer in a freezer-safe container. Freeze. When ready to eat, reheat in a toaster or conventional oven for 15 minutes at 350°F.

FULLY LOADED BREAKFAST COOKIES

PREP: 15 minutes
COOK: 25 minutes
MAKES: 1 dozen cookies

I'm always on the hunt for quick and easy ways to put breakfast on autopilot. When I made these for the first time, I knew I'd struck gold! These flavorful vegan cookies deliver protein and fiber to keep you feeling full, and are prepped in just 15 minutes. Packed with whole-grain oats and crunchy roasted and salted sunflower seeds, these chewy, soft-baked cookies are the perfect make-ahead breakfast. Bake and take them wherever you go!

Love Note

Raw or roasted, sunflower seeds are a source of vitamin E, an antioxidant that may preserve memory and cognitive function!

Ingredients

- 1½ cups mashed ripe banana (about 3 medium bananas)
- ¾ cup creamy, unsweetened natural sunflower butter, at room temperature
- ¼ cup brown sugar
- 2 cups instant oats
- ¼ cup flax meal
- 1½ teaspoons ground cinnamon
- ¼ teaspoon salt
- ¼ cup dried cranberries or blueberries
- ¼ cup roasted and salted sunflower seeds

Directions

1. Preheat the oven to 350°F. Line a large baking sheet with parchment paper.

2. In a large bowl, whisk or stir the mashed banana with the sunflower butter and brown sugar until combined into a smooth paste.

3. Add the oats, flax meal, cinnamon, salt, cranberries or blueberries, and sunflower seeds. Stir until a dough ball forms. The mixture will be sticky.

4. Use an ice-cream scoop or ¼-cup measuring cup coated with cooking spray or brushed with oil to scoop the dough into 12 portions. Using wet hands, roll each scoop into a ball, place it on the lined baking sheet, then press it into a ½-inch-thick cookie using your hand or the bottom of a glass.

5. Bake for 20 to 25 minutes, until brown on the bottom. The cookies will be dense and chewy.

6. Enjoy warm, or cool them completely and store in an airtight container at room temperature for up to 3 days, or in the freezer for up to 3 months.

Tips
- Mash the banana until it's loose and smooth.
- Swap the sunflower butter for your favorite natural nut butter.
- No dried cranberries or blueberries? Swap in your favorite dried chopped fruit.

SIMPLE
SNACKS

FRUIT AND OAT BARS

PREP: 5 minutes
COOK: 50 minutes
MAKES: 8 bars

This versatile vegan bar is packed with whole-grain oats, fruit, and nuts for a super-satisfying snack that couldn't be easier to make! I started making this recipe when we all started spending a lot more time at home during the pandemic. I use whatever ingredients I have on hand and have found endless flavor combinations—it's an incredibly adaptable recipe and perfect for weekly snack prep. My favorite flavor combinations have been fresh blackberry and almond; dried cherry and pecan; and apricot and pistachio.

Bonus: The ground flaxseed helps bind the bars and is an excellent source of plant-based omega-3 fats for heart health and of lignans, which may help reduce the risk of certain cancers.

Ingredients

- 2 cups old-fashioned oats
- 2 tablespoons ground flaxseed
- 1 tablespoon ground cinnamon
- ½ teaspoon kosher salt
- ¼ cup pure maple syrup (or brown sugar)
- 1¼ cups plant milk
- 1 cup chopped, fresh, or dried fruit such as figs, cranberries, blueberries, cherries, or apricots
- ½ cup chopped pecans or other nuts

Directions

1. Preheat the oven to 375°F. Line a 9-by-5-inch loaf pan with parchment paper.

2. Combine all the ingredients in a large bowl until well mixed. Let sit for at least 5 minutes, until some liquid is absorbed into the oats.

3. Pour the oat mixture into the pan. Bake for 45 to 50 minutes, until the center is set.

4. Remove it from the pan and set on a cooling rack. Once cool, slice it into 8 bars.

Love Note

Oats are a source of the soluble fiber beta-glucan, which has been shown to help reduce blood cholesterol.

Tips
- Full-fat coconut milk adds incredible flavor and moisture to the bars, and it's my preferred milk to use in this recipe. You can also use cashew, almond, or other plant milk with success.
- Eat within a few days at room temperature or warmed.
- Freeze the sliced bars in a freezer-safe container for up to 3 months.
- Store your ground flaxseed in the fridge or freezer for maximum shelf life.

BBQ-ROASTED BLACK-EYED PEAS

PREP: 5 minutes
COOK: 35 minutes
MAKES: 4 servings

If you're only eating black-eyed peas on New Year's Day, you have some catching up to do. These tasty little beans are an African-heritage food that's especially common throughout the South. While I love using field peas for Hoppin' John or to mix with tomatoes or greens in a salad, these roasted black-eyed peas stay in rotation.

Bonus: This protein- and iron-rich snack also happens to be a great way to use up leftover black-eyed peas—just make sure they are still firm, not mushy.

Ingredients

- 2 cups cooked firm black-eyed peas (about one [15-ounce] can, drained and rinsed)
- 2 tablespoons olive, avocado, peanut, or other neutral oil
- 2 tablespoons homemade BBQ seasoning (page 75)
- Salt, to taste

Directions

1. Preheat the oven to 400°F.

2. Spread the black-eyed peas onto a clean, lint-free dish towel or paper towels. Gently roll the peas over the towel to remove any excess moisture.

3. Once the peas are dry, spread them onto a half sheet pan in a single layer. Drizzle with the oil and sprinkle evenly with the BBQ seasoning to coat.

4. Roast on the middle rack of the oven for 25 to 35 minutes, or until the peas are browned and crisp, tossing midway. Important: Oven temperatures and moisture content can vary. Start checking the peas at the 20-minute mark to avoid burning.

5. Once done, remove the peas from the oven and let them cool on the sheet pan. Sprinkle with extra salt to taste—remember the BBQ seasoning contains salt.

6. Once completely cool, store in an airtight jar. The roasted peas will stay crispy for about 1 week.

Love Note

Black-eyed peas, or cowpeas, are a great source of iron, a key nutrient of concern if you're following a completely plant-based diet.

Tips
- ✓ Enjoy these roasted black-eyed peas fresh from the oven or as a healthy, pantry-stable snack throughout the week.
- ✓ Sprinkle the crunchy, BBQ-seasoned peas over a green salad or vegetable soup for texture and flavor.

ROSEMARY-ROASTED WALNUTS

PREP: 5 minutes
COOK: 30 minutes
SERVES: 8

Aromatic and bold, rosemary and garlic pair with walnuts in this savory and satisfying snack. I love keeping these in a mason jar to add a dose of good fats, flavor, and crunch to salads or winter soups, like my Herbed Cauliflower and White Bean Soup (page 126).

Bonus: These toasty walnuts are not just good for your taste buds but may also support heart, brain, and gut health!

Ingredients

- 2 tablespoons olive oil
- 2 tablespoons finely chopped fresh rosemary
- 1 teaspoon freshly cracked black pepper
- 1 teaspoon garlic powder
- ¾ teaspoon smoked sea salt
- 2 cups shelled walnuts

Directions

1. Preheat the oven to 300°F.
2. Whisk the olive oil, rosemary, pepper, garlic powder, and smoked sea salt in a medium bowl. Add the walnuts, and toss to coat evenly.
3. Pour the walnut mixture onto a baking sheet in a single layer. Bake for 30 minutes, stirring midway through.
4. Let cool completely on the sheet pan. Store in an airtight container at room temperature for up to a week or in the refrigerator for up to 3 months.

Love Note

Research suggests that regularly eating walnuts may increase gut-friendly bacteria for a positive impact on the microbiome.

Tips

- ✓ Be sure to use fresh walnuts to make this recipe. Taste them beforehand to make sure there are no bitter or off-flavors.
- ✓ If serving the same day, top the walnuts with lemon zest for an extra pop of flavor and color.
- ✓ Fresh rosemary is best, but you can use dried in a pinch. Be sure to toast dried rosemary in a bit of oil beforehand to wake up the flavor.
- ✓ Smoked sea salt adds a subtle smoky flavor, but you can use regular salt and smoked paprika for a similar effect.

PARMESAN ZUCCHINI CRISPS

PREP: 10 minutes
COOK: 30 minutes
MAKES: 2 servings

Use up garden-fresh zucchini for a crispy, cheesy, and savory snack or side that everyone will love. I usually eat these straight from the pan, but you can enjoy them alongside your favorite burger or main dish, or as a warm snack all on their own.

Ingredients

- 1 tablespoon extra-virgin olive oil, plus more for the pan
- 1 large zucchini, sliced in ¼-inch coins
- ¼ cup almond flour
- ¼ cup grated Parmesan cheese (or vegan Parmesan)
- 1 teaspoon garlic powder
- ¼ teaspoon black pepper
- Pinch of salt

Directions

1. Preheat the oven to 450°F. Lightly brush a baking sheet with olive oil. Set aside.

2. Press the zucchini slices between two clean dish towels or paper towels to remove excess moisture.

3. In a bowl, toss the zucchini slices in the olive oil to coat.

4. In a shallow tray, combine the almond flour, Parmesan, garlic powder, pepper, and salt. Press the zucchini slices into the almond-flour mixture, coating both sides, then transfer the slices to the prepared baking sheet.

5. Bake for 25 to 30 minutes, turning midway, until the zucchini is a toasty golden brown and crispy.

Love Note

Zucchini is 95 percent water by weight and can be eaten raw or cooked.

Tips
- ✓ Enjoy these crisps fresh from the oven for the best texture and flavor.
- ✓ Slicing the zucchini thicker will prevent the chips from becoming as crispy.

PEANUT CHILI CRUNCH POPCORN

PREP: 0 minutes
COOK: 15 minutes
SERVES: 4

I created this easy recipe at a time when chili crisp sauce was having a big moment on social media, showing up in everything from noodles to fried eggs. But people have been making and eating chili crisp sauce in and outside of China for years. Blends vary but tend to offer sweet-heat flavor with crunch from fried chili peppers, garlic, or onion. I keep a jar on hand so that this sweet, spicy, and smoky popcorn is never out of reach! Pop a batch of this crunchy treat for movie night or as an anytime snack.

Ingredients

- ¼ cup chili crunch oil, or more to taste
- ¼ cup peanut oil (or other high-heat cooking oil)
- ⅓ cup popcorn kernels
- 2 tablespoons crushed salted and roasted peanuts

Directions

1. Heat the chili oil in a small saucepan over medium-low heat until warm, about 5 minutes. Keep warm on the lowest setting until the popcorn is ready.

2. In a separate large, heavy-bottom pot with a lid, add 2 tablespoons of peanut oil and the popcorn kernels. Cover and turn the heat up to medium-high. Listen.

3. As the kernels pop, gently shake the pot to make sure all kernels are heated. Periodically open the lid (away from you) to allow steam to escape. Once the popping slows down, after about 3 minutes, remove the pot from the heat and carefully open the lid.

4. Add the popcorn to a large, wide serving bowl. Drizzle the hot popcorn with the warm chili oil while turning the bowl. Sprinkle it with the peanuts and serve immediately.

Love Note

Three cups of popcorn provide 3½ grams of fiber and a high level of polyphenols.

Tip   ✓ Use your favorite chili crunch oil. I like Lao Gan Ma Spicy Chili Crisp and Fly by Jing Sichuan Chili Crisp brands or, if I can't find those, Trader Joe's Chili Onion Crunch.

NO-BAKE ALMOND BERRY BARS

PREP: 15 minutes
COOK: 30 minutes
MAKES: 1 dozen bars

I love using dates and other fruits to create naturally sweetened snacks with a big nutritional punch. These almond-berry bars are just that. The chia seeds combine with sweet and tart raspberries for a fresh jam that naturally gels without the need for heat. The ruby-red spread sits atop a nutty, chewy crust made simply from a blend of almonds and dates. This make-ahead recipe is the perfect nutritious midday snack. Use any berries you have on hand.

Love Note

Raspberries are loaded with vitamin C and 8 grams of fiber per cup.

Ingredients

CRUST:
- 1 cup whole almonds
- 10 pitted dates, at room temperature
- 1 teaspoon cinnamon
- ½ teaspoon vanilla extract
- Pinch of kosher salt

TOPPING:
- 1 cup fresh raspberries
- ¼ teaspoon chia seeds
- 3 pitted dates
- ½ teaspoon vanilla extract
- ½ cup chopped almonds

Directions

1. **Make the crust:** Put the almonds and dates in a food processor. Pulse a few times, then process on high until the mixture forms crumb-size pieces. Scrape down the sides of the bowl. Add the cinnamon, vanilla extract, and salt. Process on high until the mixture starts to stick together or clump. Important: If your dates have started to dry out, you may need to add a splash of water for the crust to stick together.

2. Line an 8-by-8-inch baking pan with wax or parchment paper, allowing the paper to hang over the sides. Press the almond-date mixture firmly and evenly into the pan, taking care to cover the corners. Place the pan in the freezer for at least 10 minutes to set, or chill overnight in the refrigerator.

3. **Make the topping:** In a blender, puree the raspberries, chia seeds, dates, and vanilla extract until smooth.

4. Once the crust has set, spread the raspberry topping evenly over the crust. Sprinkle with the chopped almonds. Freeze for at least 30 minutes to set.

5. Once set, cut into 12 bars. Enjoy right away or store in a sealed container for up to 3 days in the refrigerator or sealed in the freezer for up to 3 months. Allow 5 to 10 minutes for frozen bars to soften slightly at room temperature before eating.

Tips
- ✓ Choose plump, moist dates. Let them warm to room temperature before processing. For a longer-lasting snack, swap the fresh raspberry topping for your favorite store-bought fruit spread.
- ✓ Swap in pecans or walnuts, in equal amounts, for the almonds.

SWEET AND SALTY PEPITA GRANOLA

PREP: 2 minutes
COOK: 20 minutes
MAKES: 6 cups

This is easily my favorite granola recipe: crunchy, sweet, salty, nutty, and even a little chewy. I shared it years ago during a cooking class and knew it was a hit when people kept tagging me on Instagram as they made it over and over at home. Though you can use any nut or seed blend, I love using pepitas—the green, shell-free seed from oilseed pumpkins— as the base (they're much easier to chew than standard white pumpkin seeds). This grain-free recipe is mostly hands-off, doubles easily, and stays fresh in the pantry for a while. So go ahead and make a big batch!

Ingredients

- 2 cups raw unsalted pepitas
- 2 cups raw unsalted sunflower seeds
- 1 cup raw unsalted slivered almonds
- ⅓ cup maple syrup
- ½ teaspoon coarse salt
- 1 cup dried tart cherries, chopped

Directions

1. Preheat the oven to 300°F. Prepare a large baking sheet (you may need two pans or to work in batches) with parchment paper or a silicone baking mat.

2. In a large bowl, stir the pepitas, sunflower seeds, almonds, and maple syrup to coat. Spread the mixture onto the prepared baking sheet(s) in a single layer. Sprinkle with salt.

3. Bake for about 25 to 30 minutes, stirring midway, until the seeds and nuts become lightly golden brown and fragrant.

4. Remove from the oven. Allow the granola to cool completely on the baking sheet. Toss in the dried cherries.

5. Store the granola in a sealed glass jar for up to 2 weeks.

Love Note

Get some z's! Pepitas are very high in magnesium, which may help promote good sleep.

Tips
✓ Lining the baking sheet keeps the maple syrup from burning and sticking.
✓ Store raw nuts and seeds in the refrigerator or freezer for extended shelf life.

SOUPS, SALADS, AND SANDWICHES

FRESH PEACH CAPRESE

PREP: 15 minutes
COOK: 0 minutes
SERVES: 4

With their naturally sweet flavor, peaches are a perfect addition to caprese salad. There may have been a time or two in testing this recipe when I enjoyed the leftovers on flatbread or with some warm bread and a glass of white wine and called that dinner. Try it for yourself. This recipe is especially delicious at the end of the summer when fresh peaches taste best.

Ingredients

- 1 pint grape or cherry tomatoes
- 2 medium peaches, pitted
- 4 ounces fresh mozzarella
- ¼ cup extra-virgin olive oil
- 2 garlic cloves, peeled and minced
- 1 tablespoon balsamic vinegar
- ½ teaspoon salt or more to taste
- ¼ teaspoon freshly cracked black pepper
- ½ teaspoon sugar (optional)
- ½ cup torn fresh basil

Directions

1. Quarter the tomatoes. Cut the peaches and mozzarella into cubes about the same size as the tomato quarters. Set aside.

2. Whisk the olive oil, garlic, balsamic vinegar, salt, pepper, and sugar, if using, in a large bowl until combined.

3. Add the cut tomatoes, peaches, and mozzarella and the basil. Toss to coat. Serve immediately.

Love Note

During tomato season, look for tomatoes of all colors and sizes. Sungold and cherry varieties add sweet flavor and beautiful color to this salad.

Tip

✓ If you're not serving the salad immediately, salt the tomatoes to reduce wateriness: Toss the quartered tomatoes in ½ teaspoon salt. Let stand for 30 minutes. Drain the liquid, and use the tomatoes per the recipe directions, eliminating the ½ teaspoon salt from the ingredients.

BROWN RICE AND CABBAGE CRUNCH SALAD

PREP: 20 minutes using cooked rice
COOK: 0 minutes
SERVES: 6

This vegan and meal-prep-friendly salad is a little sweet, a lot crunchy, and packed with flavor and nutrition. I often hear clients say, "I eat a salad but still feel hungry." That won't happen with this one. The key to a filling salad is including plenty of protein, fiber, and healthy fats—this one has it all. Edamame rises to the challenge with a whopping 18 grams of protein and 8 grams of fiber in just one cup! And the salad gets a dose of healthy fats from peanuts and olive oil. I've got you covered with this one.

Ingredients

SALAD DRESSING:
- ¼ cup extra-virgin olive oil (or plain sesame oil)
- 2 tablespoons organic toasted sesame oil
- 3 tablespoons raw organic apple cider vinegar
- 2 tablespoons coconut sugar (or maple syrup)
- ½ teaspoon coarse salt, or to taste
- ¼ teaspoon red pepper flakes
- 2 garlic cloves, peeled and grated
- 1-inch piece fresh ginger, peeled and grated
- ¼ cup peanut butter (or miso paste)

SALAD:
- 2 cups cooked brown rice
- 3 cups shredded green cabbage
- 2 cups shredded red cabbage
- 1 cup shredded carrot
- 1½ cups shelled edamame, thawed if frozen or steamed if fresh
- ½ cup roasted, salted peanuts
- 2 tablespoons chopped scallions (green onions)

Directions

1. Whisk all the salad dressing ingredients in a large bowl.

2. Add the brown rice, green and red cabbage, carrot, and edamame to the bowl. Toss to coat.

3. Top with peanuts and scallions. Serve immediately.

Tips

- ✓ If you opt for miso paste instead of peanut butter, eliminate the ½ teaspoon of salt in the dressing.
- ✓ This salad is best served right after it's dressed. However, the dressing can be made up to a week in advance so that it's ready when you are.
- ✓ Shred the cabbage and carrot by hand or use a food processor for best results. You can use (bagged) presliced cabbage, but the salad will be much drier.

STRAWBERRY, ARUGULA, AND PISTACHIO SALAD

PREP: 15 minutes
COOK: 0 minutes
SERVES: 2

This spring salad is a perfect balance of sweet, savory, crunchy, and salty. I like using arugula for a hint of peppery flavor, but strawberries are the star here. Strawberries are bursting with vitamin C, with just a cup of sliced berries meeting over 100 percent of your daily needs. Strawberries are in season from early spring to early summer and provide the perfect pop of flavor and color in this salad.

Ingredients

VINAIGRETTE:
- ¼ cup extra-virgin olive oil
- 3 tablespoons balsamic vinegar
- 1 shallot, minced
- 1 tablespoon honey
- Coarse salt, to taste
- Freshly ground black pepper, to taste

SALAD:
- 2 cups fresh strawberries, halved
- 5 ounces arugula
- ½ cup roasted, salted pistachios
- ½ cup crumbled feta (or vegan feta)

Directions

1. Whisk all the vinaigrette ingredients in a large bowl until combined.

2. Add the strawberries, arugula, pistachios, and feta. Toss to combine. Sprinkle with extra pepper and salt. Serve immediately.

Make it vegan: Use plant-based feta and swap brown sugar or date syrup for the honey.

Love Note

Pistachios provide heart-healthy fats and contain more potassium than other nuts, which can help reduce the risk of high blood pressure.

Tips
- ✓ Add grilled shrimp, salmon, or edamame for an entrée salad.
- ✓ Can't do pistachios? Roasted, salted sunflower seeds are perfect in this salad too.

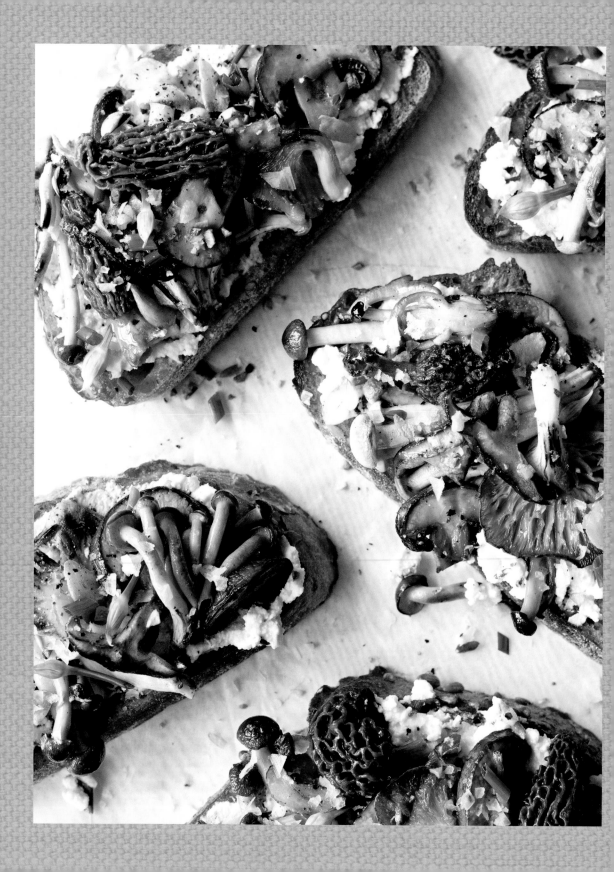

MUSHROOM RICOTTA TOAST

PREP: 5 minutes
COOK: 10 minutes
SERVES: 4

A hearty piece of toast is one of life's simple pleasures—and this one delivers. Topped with mushrooms for a savory, earthy flavor that truly satisfies, this toast can be made quickly for breakfast, lunch, or a serious snack. The chives add a pop of color, a slight onion flavor, and an elegance to the recipe. I love using crusty, rustic bread from a local bakery or a no-knead, Dutch-oven-baked bread that I make at home.

Love Note

Sourdough bread contains high levels of some nutrients like folate, which may provide some gut health benefits, and it may be better for blood sugar control, compared with other breads.

Ingredients

- 2 tablespoons olive oil, plus more for garnish
- 8 ounces baby bella or mixed mushrooms, sliced
- 2 garlic cloves, peeled and minced
- 1 tablespoon sherry vinegar
- Salt, to taste
- Black pepper, to taste
- ½ cup ricotta (or vegan ricotta), at room temperature
- ¼ cup chopped fresh chives, plus more for garnish
- 4 thick slices of your favorite rustic bread, toasted

Directions

1. Heat the olive oil in a large skillet over medium heat. Add the mushrooms. Sauté until the mushrooms caramelize, about 7 to 8 minutes. Just before all the liquid evaporates, add the garlic and sherry vinegar. Season with salt and pepper.

2. While the mushrooms are cooking, mix the ricotta and the chives.

3. To assemble the toasts, spread 2 tablespoons of the herbed ricotta on each slice of toasted bread. Top with ¼ of the mushrooms. Sprinkle with chives and a drizzle of olive oil, if desired.

Tips

✓ For the best flavor and texture, use a crusty whole-grain bread, sourdough, or pain au levain.
✓ For extra flavor, pan-toast the bread in olive oil instead of using the toaster. Do this before cooking the mushrooms.
✓ Taste the ricotta before seasoning the mushrooms, and adjust the salt accordingly.
✓ Use a cast-iron skillet to cook the mushrooms for ultimate caramelization.
✓ If you don't have fresh chives, you can substitute dried ones or top with another fresh herb such as thyme.

CHICKPEA AND RICE SOUP

PREP: 15 minutes
COOK: 35 minutes
SERVES: 4

Think chicken noodle soup but with chickpeas and rice! This hearty soup is what you'll want to curl up with on a chilly fall evening. It's also what you'll want to serve to your friends and family who could use a little comfort!

Ingredients

- 2 tablespoons extra-virgin olive oil
- 1 medium white or yellow onion, diced
- 2 medium celery ribs, chopped
- 2 medium carrots, peeled and chopped
- 2 garlic cloves, peeled and minced
- ½ teaspoon ground black pepper
- 1 cup uncooked long-grain white or brown rice
- 8 cups low-sodium vegetable or chicken broth
- 2 cups cooked chickpeas (or one [15-ounce] can, drained and rinsed)
- Parmesan rind (or 1 teaspoon vegan soup base, vegan bouillon, or white miso)
- 1 teaspoon salt, or more to taste
- 1 bay leaf
- ½ lemon, juiced
- 2 tablespoons finely chopped fresh parsley

Directions

1. Put the oil in a large stockpot over medium-high heat. Add the onion, celery, and carrots. Cook for about 5 minutes until the onion is translucent.

2. Add the garlic, pepper, and rice. Cook until the rice is slightly toasted, about 5 minutes.

3. Add the broth, chickpeas, Parmesan rind (or vegan alternative), salt, and bay leaf. Bring to a boil. Cover and reduce the heat to medium-low. Simmer for 15 to 18 minutes for white rice, or about 35 minutes for brown rice, or until the rice is tender.

4. Remove from the heat. Use tongs to remove the bay leaf and Parmesan rind (if using). Stir in the lemon juice. Taste for seasoning, adding extra salt if needed. Serve immediately topped with fresh parsley.

Important serving notes: Serve this soup right away. If you have leftovers or want to serve it later:

- **Option 1:** Strain the broth from the soup and store separately in the refrigerator. As the soup sits, the rice will continue to absorb the liquid, making for more of a stew than a soup. Straining will keep the rice from plumping too much.

- **Option 2:** Omit the uncooked rice and add seasoned cooked rice to the soup just before serving.

 Tip ✓ Use a high-quality broth that you love for this recipe.

WARM ROASTED BROCCOLI SALAD

PREP: 10 minutes
COOK: 10 minutes
SERVES: 6

Broccoli salad is a thing in the South. It's usually served cold with raw broccoli, raisins, bacon, and a creamy dressing. This version uses grapes instead of raisins and roasted broccoli—my spin on that traditional recipe. To continue with the southern take and to add a little crunch, I included toasted pecans. I promise that your friends will want you to bring this one to the table next time!

Love Note

A southern staple, pecans add crunch and lots of heart-healthy monounsaturated fats and other important nutrients like fiber and copper.

Ingredients

VINAIGRETTE:
- ¼ cup extra-virgin olive oil
- 2 tablespoons balsamic vinegar
- 1 tablespoon honey (or date syrup or brown sugar if vegan)
- 1 small shallot, minced
- ¼ teaspoon kosher salt
- ⅛ teaspoon ground black pepper

SALAD:
- 6 cups bite-size broccoli florets (about 2 medium heads)
- 2 tablespoons extra-virgin olive oil
- 1½ cups halved red or black grapes
- ½ cup toasted pecans, chopped

Directions

1. Preheat the oven to 400°F.

2. In a jar with a lid, combine all the vinaigrette ingredients. Shake until blended and set aside.

3. Spread the broccoli florets in a single layer on a sheet pan. Drizzle with the olive oil and toss to coat. Roast for 12 to 15 minutes, until the broccoli starts to caramelize but retains its pleasant green color. Remove from the oven.

4. In a large bowl, toss the warm broccoli, grapes, and pecans with the vinaigrette. Serve warm.

Tips
- ✓ If you don't have a shallot, use 1 clove garlic, minced.
- ✓ Break the broccoli florets into similarly sized pieces for even roasting and to make the salad easier to eat.

Love Note

Raw garlic cloves contain allicin, a sulfur compound that is responsible for many of garlic's anti-inflammatory effects.

HERBED CAULIFLOWER AND WHITE BEAN SOUP

PREP: 15 minutes
COOK: 35 minutes
SERVES: 4

Silky, smooth, and nourishing, this soup is perfect for a chilly winter night. White beans are an excellent way to add a creamy texture to vegetable soups and sauces while also boosting fiber and protein. I use miso for that umami flavor you'd typically get from smoked meat. All of this together makes for a simple but savory soup that's perfect served with warm crusty bread or a sprinkle of toasted walnuts for crunch and a dose of good fats.

Ingredients

- ¼ cup extra-virgin olive oil, plus more for topping
- 1 medium onion, chopped
- 4 garlic cloves, peeled and smashed
- 1 tablespoon fresh rosemary (or 1 teaspoon dried)
- 5 cups cauliflower florets (about 1 medium head)
- 1 (15-ounce) can low-sodium navy beans, drained and rinsed (or 1¾ cups cooked)
- 4 cups quality broth
- 2 tablespoons white miso
- ½ to 1 teaspoon salt
- ½ teaspoon black pepper
- Chopped walnuts, for topping
- Big garlicky croutons, for topping

Directions

1. In a large stockpot, heat the olive oil over medium heat.

2. Sauté the onion for about 5 to 7 minutes, until translucent. Add the garlic and rosemary. Cook for another 1 to 2 minutes.

3. Stir in the cauliflower florets, beans, broth, miso, ½ teaspoon of the salt, and the pepper. Bring to a boil. Reduce the heat to a simmer. Cover and cook until the cauliflower is tender, about 15 to 20 minutes.

4. Puree the soup in the pot using an immersion blender. If the soup is too thick, thin it with hot broth. Taste and adjust the seasonings based on the broth you've used. Start with another ½ teaspoon salt and add more if needed.

5. Top with a drizzle of olive oil and the walnuts and croutons.

Tips

- ✓ Navy beans have a mild flavor and blend well for a smooth and creamy finish. You can also use great northern beans or cannellini beans.
- ✓ If you use dried rosemary, optimize its flavor. "Bloom" the dried herbs by adding them to the oil in step 1. Cook for about 30 seconds before adding the onion.
- ✓ Adjust the salt based on the type of beans, miso, and broth to avoid an overly salted soup.

SMASHED CHICKPEA SALAD SANDWICH

PREP: 10 minutes using canned chickpeas
COOK: 0 minutes
MAKES: 4 sandwiches

I keep a variety of canned beans on hand for quick meals, and chickpeas are always in the pantry. This colorful salad is a go-to recipe. Smashing the ingredients helps pull the flavorful oils and juices from the olives, onions, peppers, and garlic for a mix that can easily be stuffed into a lettuce wrap or between two slices of bread. This recipe can easily be doubled, and gets even better overnight—the perfect weekly meal prep and lunch box meal!

Ingredients

- 1 (15-ounce) can low-sodium chickpeas, drained and rinsed (or 1¾ cups cooked)
- ½ small red bell pepper, diced small
- ½ small red onion, diced small
- 2 tablespoons pitted kalamata olives, diced small
- 2 garlic cloves, peeled and minced
- 1 small lemon, juiced
- 2 tablespoons extra-virgin olive oil
- Salt, to taste
- Black pepper, to taste
- ¼ cup chopped fresh flat-leaf parsley
- Your favorite bread, crackers, or lettuce cups

Directions

1. In a medium bowl, mash the chickpeas, bell pepper, onion, olives, and garlic using a potato masher or fork until the chickpeas start to clump together but the mixture is still chunky.

2. Stir in the lemon juice, olive oil, salt, and black pepper. Sprinkle with parsley.

3. Portion the chickpea salad evenly onto bread or crackers or into lettuce cups to serve.

Tips

✓ Draining and rinsing canned beans with cool running water can reduce sodium by up to 41 percent.
✓ Feel free to swap in any color bell pepper and use a sweet or white onion instead of red.
✓ Add a dash of hot sauce or smash in some jalapeños for a little heat.

PESTO WHITE BEAN VEGGIE WRAP

PREP: 5 minutes with prepared pesto
COOK: 20 minutes
MAKES: 4 wraps

Though you *could* just eat cauliflower, tomatoes, and white beans dressed with pesto, stuffing them into a wrap is a little more fun. And who doesn't love a handheld lunch? Make a big batch of the filling using a sheet pan to serve these up with ease. The white beans provide an impressive 10 grams of heart-healthy fiber in one cup and plenty of protein to keep you feeling full.

Ingredients

- 1 (15-ounce) can cannellini beans, drained, rinsed, and dried
- 2 cups bite-size cauliflower florets (about ½ medium head)
- 1 cup grape tomatoes, whole
- ⅓ cup vegan or kale pesto, at room temperature (page 72)
- 4 burrito-size wraps (any variety: whole grain, grain-free, etc.)
- 2 cups fresh arugula

Directions

1. Preheat the oven to 400°F. Line a baking sheet with parchment paper.

2. Taking care to keep the beans intact, toss the beans, cauliflower florets, and tomatoes with the pesto in a large bowl.

3. Pour the mixture onto the prepared baking sheet, keeping plenty of space between the vegetables. Roast in the oven for 20 minutes, carefully tossing midway.

4. Meanwhile warm the wraps by toasting them on the stovetop or in a dry skillet—or in the microwave covered with a microwave-safe plate or clean, damp napkin—until pliable.

5. Add ½ cup of arugula to each wrap. Top with ¼ of the warm pesto-roasted vegetables. Tuck. Roll. Serve. Enjoy warm or at room temperature.

Love Note

Women should aim for at least 25 grams and men 38 grams of fiber per day.

Tip   ✓ If serving the next day, add a layer of hummus to the wrap as a barrier to prevent it from getting soggy, or wait to fill the wrap right before eating it.

AUTUMN HARVEST SALAD

PREP: 30 minutes (5 minutes if using precooked farro)
COOK: 30 minutes
SERVES: 4

This salad of apples and cool-weather greens celebrates hearty fall flavors and is perfect for taking on the go. I love adding grains to salads to make them more substantial. Farro is an ancient grain that provides a pleasant nutty flavor and chewy texture. Plus, it's high in fiber and delivers a healthy dose of essential vitamins and minerals such as magnesium, zinc, and niacin.

Love Note

Research suggests that eating apples might reduce the risk of numerous chronic diseases, including stroke, heart disease, and type 2 diabetes.

Ingredients

SALAD:
- 1 cup uncooked farro (2 cups cooked)
- 2 medium apples, diced
- ½ cup toasted pecan halves
- 4 cups baby spinach or kale

VINAIGRETTE:
- 3 tablespoons extra-virgin olive oil
- 3 tablespoons raw apple cider vinegar
- 1 tablespoon maple syrup or more for desired sweetness
- ½ small shallot, minced
- ½ tablespoon Dijon mustard
- ¼ teaspoon salt
- Pinch of black pepper, or more to taste

Directions

1. **Cook the farro.** Bring a large pot of salted water to a boil. Add the uncooked farro and boil until al dente, about 30 minutes. Drain well. (If prepping for later, store in the refrigerator.)

2. **Make the vinaigrette.** In a large bowl, add all the vinaigrette ingredients and whisk until combined.

3. **Assemble the salad.** Toss the diced apples, pecans, and farro in the vinaigrette until well coated. Add the spinach or kale and toss. Plate and serve.

Make it ahead: Using 4 large mason jars, pour ¼ of the vinaigrette into each jar, then layer in the farro, apples, pecans, and spinach or kale, in that order. When you're ready to eat, pour into a bowl and enjoy!

Tip ✓ Hardy Tuscan kale (aka dinosaur or lacinato kale) works well if making this recipe ahead of time. For ease, use prewashed baby greens from the produce aisle. Add baby spinach or kale just before eating to keep it from wilting.

PESTO CHICKPEA BOWLS

PREP: 10 minutes using cooked quinoa
COOK: 10 minutes
SERVES: 4

Get vegetables, protein, and fiber in this flavor-packed work-from-wherever lunch bowl. I use the kale pesto (page 72) for this recipe, but feel free to use whatever you have on hand. To have these bowls ready for quick lunches, make a batch each of quinoa, soft-boiled eggs, and pesto ahead of time so all that's left to do is a quick assembly when you're ready to eat.

Love Note

Chickpeas, or garbanzo beans, are chock-full of plant-based protein, providing almost 15 grams in a one-cup serving.

Ingredients

- 2 cups cooked quinoa*
- 4 large eggs
- ⅓ cup kale pesto (page 72)
- 1¾ cups cooked chickpeas (one [15-ounce] can, drained and rinsed)
- 1 cup grape tomatoes, halved
- Salt, to taste
- Freshly cracked black pepper, to taste
- Parmesan, for topping
- Scallions, for topping
- Shredded carrots, for topping

Directions

1. Cook quinoa according to package directions or per note below, or use leftover quinoa or rice.

2. Soft-boil the eggs by slowly lowering them into boiling water. Set a timer for 6 minutes. When the time is up, transfer the eggs to an ice bath and let them cool. When ready to use, peel the eggs and slice them in half lengthwise.

3. Place the pesto in a medium skillet over medium-low heat. Add the chickpeas, toss to coat, and heat them through, about 2 to 3 minutes.

4. To assemble the bowls, place ½ cup quinoa in the bottom of a bowl. Top with about ½ cup chickpeas, ¼ cup grape tomatoes, and 1 soft-boiled egg, and sprinkle with salt and pepper. Repeat for the other bowls. Top each with Parmesan, scallions, and shredded carrots or other vegetables.

* To cook quinoa: Rinse 1 cup quinoa under cool running water. Drain. Toast quinoa over medium heat in a saucepan to evaporate any excess water. Add 1¾ cups water or broth and bring to a boil. Reduce the heat to low, and cook covered for 15 minutes. Let stand, covered, for 15 minutes. Fluff and eat, cool and refrigerate, or freeze until you're ready to make these bowls.

Make it vegan: Skip the eggs and use vegan pesto (page 72).

Tips
✓ No chickpeas on hand? Swap in cannellini beans.
✓ Not into quinoa? Try barley, thick-cut or steel-cut oats, rice, or even cauliflower rice in its place.

BLACK BEAN AND CHEDDAR BURGERS

PREP: 15 minutes
COOK: 10 minutes using cooked beans
MAKES: 4 burgers

I love a black bean burger. This one takes the earthy flavor of beans up a notch with smoky paprika and a splash of soy sauce. The oats give the burgers a nice crust and add an extra dose of fiber. But possibly the most sought-after trait? This stick-to-your-ribs burger doesn't fall apart—it's perfect for pan-frying or the grill. Make the patties ahead of time for an easy weeknight meal.

Love Note

Black beans are an excellent source of fiber, iron, and magnesium. Black beans get their rich color from anthocyanins, antioxidant compounds that might offer a heart-healthy boost.

Ingredients

- 2 cups cooked black beans, cooking liquid reserved (or one [15-ounce] can, drained, with liquid reserved, and rinsed)
- ½ cup finely chopped mushrooms (1½ ounces)
- ½ cup rolled oats, pulsed into a coarse flour
- 2 garlic cloves, peeled and minced
- 1 tablespoon soy sauce
- 1 teaspoon onion powder
- ½ teaspoon smoked paprika
- 2 tablespoons olive, avocado, or other neutral oil
- 4 slices cheddar cheese (or vegan cheddar), about 1 ounce each
- 4 hamburger buns, sliced and toasted, or lettuce wraps
- Chipotle mayo, for topping (page 71)
- Avocado, for topping
- Lettuce, for topping
- Tomato, sliced, for topping
- Onion, sliced, for topping

Directions

1. In a medium bowl, mash the black beans, mushrooms, pulsed oats, garlic, soy sauce, onion powder, and smoked paprika using a potato masher or fork until well combined.

2. Add the reserved black bean liquid 1 tablespoon at a time, as needed, until the mixture sticks together to easily form a ball. Shape into four even-size patties.

3. Heat the oil in a large skillet over medium-high heat.

4. Cook on one side for 3 minutes. Flip, add a slice of cheddar, cover, and cook for 2 minutes more or until the cheese melts and starts to crisp around the edges.

5. Serve on toasted buns or wrapped in lettuce, topped with the chipotle mayo, avocado, lettuce, tomato, and onion.

Tips
- ✓ Be mindful of saltiness. Choose canned black beans with a lower sodium level so you can control the flavor fate of your burger. When testing this recipe, I used canned black beans with 140 milligrams of sodium per serving.
- ✓ Use a small dry blender or mini food processor to pulse rolled oats into flour. No need to buy oat flour.
- ✓ Prep and refrigerate these burgers up to 2 days ahead of time or cook immediately.

WATERMELON SALAD WITH HONEY-LIME VINAIGRETTE

PREP: 25 minutes
COOK: 0 minutes
SERVES: 8

I like my watermelon cold and plain. Sometimes with salt. But every now and again I'll get a little fancy and start experimenting with leftovers. This salad is one of those. It's cool and refreshing and the perfect pairing with fajitas or tacos, or with salty, crispy tortilla chips. Watermelon is in season from about May to September, so serve this recipe at your summer cookouts and picnics!

Ingredients

- 1 lime, zested and juiced (2 tablespoons juice and 1 teaspoon zest)
- 2 tablespoons extra-virgin olive oil or avocado oil
- ½ teaspoon coarse salt, divided
- 2 teaspoons honey
- 4 cups watermelon cubes, cut into 1-inch cubes
- 1 medium cucumber, seeded and cut into 1-inch cubes
- 1 small red onion, diced
- 1 medium jalapeño pepper, seeded and minced
- ½ cup cotija cheese
- ¼ cup chopped fresh cilantro

Directions

1. Whisk the lime juice, olive oil, a ¼ teaspoon of the salt, and the honey in a large bowl until smooth.

2. Add the watermelon, cucumber, onion, jalapeño, lime zest, and the remaining ¼ teaspoon of salt. Toss to coat.

3. Top with the cheese and cilantro. Serve immediately.

Make it vegan: Use plant-based queso fresco or feta for the cotija and swap in vegan granulated sugar for the honey.

Love Note

Hydrating and sweet, watermelon is rich in vitamins A and C plus lycopene, which may help promote heart health.

Tips

✓ Be ready to eat this one right away. The cucumber and watermelon are more than 90 percent water, so this salad gets watery as it sits. Eat it soon after prep.
✓ Don't have cucumber? Replace it with more watermelon.
✓ Not adding cheese? You'll want to add a little extra salt to balance the flavor.

BLACK BEAN AND SPINACH QUESADILLAS

PREP: 5 minutes
COOK: 15 minutes
MAKES: 4 quesadillas

Remember that viral folded-quesadilla recipe that took over the internet a few years ago? Well, I never stopped making it. You can absolutely fold yours just once for a traditional quesadilla shape, but with this method you have options! This recipe combines iron-rich spinach and black beans for a flavorful and satisfying combo that, when served with salsa, becomes a nutrient powerhouse.

Love Note

Add some salsa to the mix. The vitamin C from the tomatoes will help you absorb more iron from the spinach and black beans!

Ingredients

- 1 tablespoon olive or avocado oil, plus more for the skillet
- ¼ cup red onion, diced
- 1 teaspoon taco seasoning (page 75)
- 2 cups cooked black beans (about one [15-ounce can], drained and rinsed)
- 4 soft 8-inch tortillas
- 2 cups fresh baby spinach, chopped
- 2 ounces shredded cheddar or Monterey Jack cheese (or vegan cheddar or Monterey Jack)
- Toppings: avocado, chipotle mayo (page 71) or sour cream, salsa, and lettuce

Directions

1. **Make the filling.** In a medium skillet, heat the olive oil and sauté the onion over medium heat for about 3 to 5 minutes, until soft. Add the taco seasoning and cook for 1 to 2 minutes, stirring frequently. Add the beans, and cook until heated through. Lightly mash ¼ of the beans slightly with the back of a fork. Set aside but keep warm.

2. **Fold the tortillas (as pictured).** Make one cut up from the edge to the center of each tortilla. Add ¼ cup chopped spinach to the bottom left and upper right corners of the tortilla. Spread ¼ of the bean mixture on the top left corner and ½ ounce cheese to the bottom right corner of the tortilla. Fold the spinach over the beans and work clockwise, folding the last quarter over the cheese. **Single-fold option:** Layer the cheese, bean mixture, and spinach on one half of the tortilla. Fold the other side over to create a half-moon shape.

3. **Toast the tortillas.** Heat 1 teaspoon of oil in a large skillet or griddle. Place the folded tortilla in the skillet, cheese side down, for 3 minutes, until golden and toasty. Press the tortilla with a cast-iron pan or a foil-wrapped brick or heavy can. Turn and cook for another 3 minutes until crispy. Repeat with each filled tortilla. Serve warm with the desired toppings.

Tips
✓ Use your favorite tortilla. Whole-grain, grain-free, and regular flour tortillas all work well.
✓ You can use leftover cooked spinach or frozen spinach that's been thawed and drained.

MUSHROOM CHEESESTEAK

PREP: 10 minutes
COOK: 15 minutes
SERVES: 4

Savory with the flavors and textures of a Philly cheesesteak but made from plants, this sandwich is for mushroom- and meat-lovers alike. The key to this recipe is using a hot pan to caramelize the onion, peppers, and mushrooms in order to bring out the natural sweetness and add a ton of flavor. I promise, you won't miss the meat.

Love Note

Mushrooms are one of the few food sources of vitamin D_2, which plays a role in a healthy immune system and maintains bone health.

Tips

✓ Use a large (12-inch) skillet with a lid. This will give the vegetables and mushrooms plenty of space to caramelize, rather than steam, in the pan.
✓ Slice the onion and bell pepper about the same thickness for even cooking.
✓ Planning for leftovers? Store the mushroom, bell pepper, and onion mixture separate from the rolls. The mixture will keep in the fridge for 2 to 3 days. Toast the rolls and reheat the mushroom mixture for a fresh sandwich.

Ingredients

- 2 tablespoons butter, melted
- 1 garlic clove, peeled and minced
- 4 split-top 6-inch rolls
- 2 tablespoons olive oil, divided
- 1 large sweet onion, sliced
- 1 green bell pepper, sliced
- ½ teaspoon salt, divided
- ½ teaspoon black pepper, divided
- 1 pound baby bella mushrooms, thickly sliced
- ½ teaspoon garlic powder
- 8 slices (4 ounces) provolone cheese
- French fries, chips, or vegetables, for serving

Directions

1. Combine the melted butter and garlic in a small bowl. Brush the garlic butter onto the cut sides of the rolls. Place the rolls on a baking sheet, cut side up, and broil on high on the top rack of your oven until the rolls are toasted to a golden color, 1 or 2 minutes. Set aside.

2. Heat 1 tablespoon of the olive oil in a large skillet over medium-high heat. Add the onion, bell pepper, and ¼ teaspoon of the salt and black pepper. Sauté, stirring occasionally, until the pepper slices are slightly charred and the onion slices have softened, about 5 to 7 minutes. Transfer to a plate and set aside.

3. Heat the remaining 1 tablespoon of oil in the skillet. Add the sliced mushrooms in a single layer. Sprinkle with the garlic powder and remaining ¼ teaspoon of salt and black pepper. Cook undisturbed for about 3 minutes, until the mushrooms start turning golden brown underneath and release some of their liquid. Flip, reduce the heat to medium, and continue cooking for 5 to 8 more minutes, until all moisture has evaporated and the mushrooms are caramelized to a dark brown color.

4. Add the sautéed onion and bell pepper back to the pan. Toss to combine. Reduce the heat to low. Use a spatula to section the vegetables into 4 equal mounds in the skillet. Top each evenly with a slice of cheese. Cover the skillet with a lid until the cheese melts, about 1 minute.

5. Spoon each section of vegetables onto one of the rolls. Serve warm solo or with a side of fries, chips, or veggies.

ROASTED CARROT SOUP

PREP: 5 minutes
COOK: 40 minutes
SERVES: 4

When soup season rolls around, put this one at the top of your list. Made with caramelized carrots, sweet onion, and a host of warm spices, it's like a nourishing hug in a bowl. This soup is heavy on the coriander and ginger—both antioxidant-rich spices that perfectly complement the naturally sweet carrots. Enjoy this velvety soup with a drizzle of olive oil or yogurt on top alongside some warm, crusty bread.

Love Note

Carrots are very high in beta-carotene, and cooking them helps your body absorb more of it–up to 6.5 times more!

Tips

✓ Use your favorite homemade or high-quality store-bought broth or broth made from bouillon. Choose vegetable broth to keep it vegan or chicken broth for a more savory flavor.
✓ Adjust the salt based on your broth.

Ingredients

- 1 medium sweet onion (I prefer Vidalia), cut into large chunks
- 1 pound carrots, peeled and sliced into 2-inch chunks
- 4 tablespoons extra-virgin olive oil, divided
- 1 teaspoon salt, divided
- 2 garlic cloves, peeled and smashed
- 1-inch piece fresh ginger, peeled and grated (about 1 teaspoon)
- 1 teaspoon ground coriander
- ¼ teaspoon crushed red chili flakes
- 3 cups quality broth, warmed
- Fresh cilantro, for garnish
- Yogurt, for garnish
- Peanuts, for garnish

Directions

1. Preheat the oven to 425°F.

2. Spread the onion and carrot chunks, keeping the onion layers intact, on a sheet pan in a single layer. Coat evenly with 1 tablespoon of the olive oil and ½ teaspoon of the salt. Roast until the carrots are fork-tender and caramelized, about 35 to 40 minutes.

3. During the last 5 minutes of roasting, bloom the spices. Add the remaining 3 tablespoons of olive oil and the garlic to a saucepan over medium heat. Cook the garlic for about 1 minute. Add the ginger, coriander, and red chili flakes. Cook for 1 to 2 minutes, stirring frequently. The spices should be pleasantly fragrant, but not browned.

4. Put the roasted carrots and onion in a blender, taking care to include the caramelized (brown) bits from the sheet pan. Add the warm broth, the oil-spice mixture, and the remaining ½ teaspoon of salt. Vent the blender lid or use a kitchen towel to cover the lid opening to allow steam to escape. Puree the soup until smooth and creamy. Taste and adjust for seasoning.

5. Serve warm. Top with the cilantro, yogurt, and peanuts, or a drizzle of olive oil.

MOSTLY
MEATLESS
MAINS

PEANUT STEW

PREP: 10 minutes
COOK: 30 minutes
SERVES: 6

This flavorful stew is inspired by West African groundnut stew. It's filled with sweet potatoes and greens that are simmered in a fragrant broth made of tomato, peanuts, onion, and fresh ginger. Commonly served over rice or with another starch, this is the ultimate comfort food. For the best flavor, roast and grind your own peanuts, or make sure your peanut butter is fresh, since it's the dominant flavor in this recipe.

Love Note

Technically a legume, peanuts have more protein per ounce than other nuts.

Ingredients

- 2 tablespoons peanut or olive oil
- 1 medium onion, diced
- 4 garlic cloves, peeled and minced
- 2-inch piece fresh ginger, peeled and minced
- ½ teaspoon smoked paprika
- ¼ to ½ teaspoon crushed red pepper flakes, to taste
- 3 tablespoons tomato paste
- 1 pound sweet potatoes, peeled and cubed (about 3 cups)
- 1 (14.5-ounce) can crushed tomatoes
- 2 cups vegetable broth
- ½ cup unsweetened smooth natural peanut butter
- ½ teaspoon salt
- ¼ teaspoon black pepper
- 5 ounces baby kale or spinach
- Cooked rice or fonio (at least 2 cups), for serving
- Chopped cilantro or parsley, for garnish
- Roasted salted peanuts, for garnish

Directions

1. Heat the oil in a large, heavy-bottomed pot over medium heat. Add the onion, garlic, ginger, smoked paprika, and red pepper flakes. Cook, stirring occasionally, until the onion is soft, about 5 minutes. Stir in the tomato paste and cook for about 1 minute. Add the cubed sweet potatoes, crushed tomatoes, broth, peanut butter, salt, and black pepper. Cook on medium heat for about 20 minutes, stirring occasionally, until the sweet potatoes are tender but not soft.

2. Add the kale or spinach and cook for another 3 to 5 minutes, until the greens are just wilted but retain their color.

3. Serve with rice or fonio and top with cilantro or parsley and roasted peanuts.

Tips
- ✓ You can also use regular kale or collard greens. Thinly slice or chop these hardy greens and add them at the same time as the sweet potatoes.
- ✓ Adjust the seasoning based on the saltiness and seasoning of the broth.
- ✓ Remember to use natural, unsweetened peanut butter. The ingredient list should have only peanuts and maybe salt.
- ✓ For more protein, add cooked red or kidney beans, tofu, or chicken to the stew.

SHRIMP SUCCOTASH

PREP: 15 minutes
COOK: 25 minutes
SERVES: 8

Succotash is a Native American dish that marries corn and beans. In the South, it's common to combine garden-fresh sweet corn, lima beans, and okra with a small amount of bacon for flavoring. Succotash is typically served as a side dish, but adding shrimp to the mix makes it fit for a main. Making this recipe brought back fond memories of sitting on the porch with my grandma shucking corn and shelling butter beans in the summer. Honoring that tradition, I am always on the lookout for the best ingredients from local farmers for recipes like these.

Tips

✓ Ingredient quality makes a huge difference with this recipe. Fresh corn, tomatoes, and okra significantly impact the sweetness and overall flavor balance.

✓ Thaw frozen corn before adding it to the skillet. Then it won't reduce the temperature of the pan.

✓ Missing the smoky bacon flavor? Try smoked salt or add a sprinkle of smoked paprika to the oil before sautéing the onion.

✓ Limit stirring once the okra is in the skillet. Overcooked okra = slimy succotash.

✓ Okra may be difficult to find fresh, and it is also highly perishable, so buy it fresh with the intention to use it within a few days.

Ingredients

- 2 cups fresh or frozen baby lima or butter beans (10 ounces)
- 2 tablespoons olive oil, divided
- 1 pound medium shrimp, peeled and deveined
- 1 cup chopped sweet onion (1 small)
- 2 cups sliced fresh okra
- 3 cups fresh sweet corn kernels (about 4 ears) or thawed and drained frozen corn kernels
- 3 garlic cloves, peeled and minced
- 1½ teaspoons salt, plus more to taste
- ½ teaspoon black pepper, plus more to taste
- 2 tablespoons butter (or vegan butter)
- 1½ cups sliced grape tomatoes (about 6 ounces)
- Fresh parsley, for garnish

Directions

1. Put the lima beans in a small pot with just enough water to cover. Cook over medium heat for about 10 minutes, until the beans are heated through but not soft or mushy.

2. Heat 1 tablespoon of the oil over medium heat in a large skillet. Season the shrimp with salt and pepper and sauté, about 3 minutes per side, until the shrimp are cooked through. Remove from the skillet and set aside.

3. Heat the remaining 1 tablespoon of oil in the skillet. Sauté the onion until softened, about 5 minutes. Add the okra, corn, garlic, salt, pepper, butter, and cooked lima beans to the skillet. Cook for about 5 minutes, until everything is heated through. Add the shrimp back to the skillet, along with the tomatoes, if using. Serve warm garnished with parsley.

Make it vegan: Omit the shrimp and use vegan butter. Since this recipe has lima beans, you'll still have a complete, protein-rich meal.

BLENDED CHICKEN AND MUSHROOM MEATBALLS

PREP: 10 minutes
COOK: 20 minutes
MAKES: 12 meatballs

Transitioning to a plant-forward way of eating? This recipe is a flavorful way to start incorporating more plant-based ingredients into everyday meals. Adding chopped mushrooms to meatballs not only enhances the incredible savory flavor and moisture, but it also provides a big fiber boost. And you can use this technique to do the same for burgers, taco filling, pasta sauce, or chili.

Love Note

Mushrooms are a good source of three different B vitamins, which give you energy.

Ingredients

- 8 ounces mushrooms
- 1 onion, quartered
- 1 pound ground chicken
- 1 large egg
- 1 tablespoon olive oil
- 1 teaspoon salt
- 1 teaspoon grated fresh ginger
- ¼ teaspoon crushed red pepper flakes
- ½ cup panko

Directions

1. Preheat the oven to 400°F. Position one rack near the top about 1 to 2 inches from the broiler and one rack in the center of the oven. Spray a large baking sheet with olive oil.

2. Process the mushrooms in a food processor until finely chopped. Transfer to a large bowl and set aside. Without cleaning the food processor bowl, process the onion until finely chopped or minced. Using a clean, lint-free kitchen towel, squeeze any excess liquid from the minced onion.

3. In the bowl with the chopped mushrooms, combine the chicken, ½ cup minced onion, egg, olive oil, salt, ginger, red pepper flakes, and panko.

4. Using gloved or wet hands and a scoop, portion 12 even meatballs onto the prepared baking sheet.

5. Bake for about 20 minutes, until the meatballs start to brown and register an internal temperature of 175°F.

6. For additional color, broil the meatballs for 1 to 2 minutes under the broiler. Serve warm with honey pepper broccoli (page 190) and rice or noodles, or enjoy with peanut sauce (page 70) and a sprinkle of scallions.

Tips

- ✓ Swap in ground turkey or beef for the chicken.
- ✓ Be sure to finely chop the mushrooms. Large pieces will cause the meatballs to fall apart.
- ✓ Try shiitake, portobello, or a mixture of your favorite, most flavorful mushrooms.
- ✓ Make burgers instead of meatballs: Use equal amounts finely chopped mushrooms and ground beef or turkey for a burger that is juicy, full of savory flavor, and higher in fiber.

CREAMY ROASTED RED PEPPER PASTA

PREP: 10 minutes
COOK: 30 minutes (plus overnight soak)
SERVES: 4

Almonds deliver a creamy texture to sauces and soups when they are soaked and blended. Roasting peppers, garlic, and cauliflower sweetens the pot and adds rich flavor to this easy, vegetable-rich pasta sauce. This sauce reminds me a bit of romesco, the flavorful Spanish sauce made by combining charred red bell peppers and tomatoes with almonds, smoked paprika, and vinegar or lemon to serve with potatoes or meat.

Love Note

Red bell peppers are one of the best sources of vitamin C, though roasting reduces the amount.

Ingredients

- 4 red bell peppers, quartered, stems and seeds removed
- 4 garlic cloves, peeled
- ¼ cup plus 2 tablespoons extra-virgin olive oil, divided
- 4 cups cauliflower florets (1 small head)
- 8 ounces pasta
- ½ lemon, juiced
- 1 teaspoon dried basil or ¼ cup torn fresh basil leaves
- ½ cup almonds, soaked overnight and drained
- ½ teaspoon salt
- ¼ teaspoon freshly cracked black pepper, plus more for garnish
- Toasted almonds, for garnish
- Fresh basil, for garnish

Directions

1. Preheat the oven to 400°F. Place the bell peppers and garlic cloves on a baking sheet. Drizzle with 1 tablespoon of the olive oil and salt and pepper to taste. On a separate baking sheet, toss the cauliflower florets with 1 tablespoon of the olive oil and salt and pepper to taste. Roast both for 25 to 30 minutes, until vegetables are tender and slightly charred.

2. During the last 10 minutes of roasting, cook the pasta in salted boiling water according to package directions. Reserve at least ½ cup of the pasta water for the sauce.

3. In a high-speed blender or food processor, blend the roasted bell peppers (skin on) and garlic with the remaining ¼ cup of the olive oil, the lemon juice, basil, almonds, salt, and pepper. Add the reserved pasta water, 1 or 2 tablespoons at a time, to thin the sauce as needed. Taste and adjust the seasoning.

4. Return the hot, drained pasta to the pot. Toss with the sauce and roasted cauliflower until combined. Garnish with extra olive oil and black pepper and the toasted almonds and fresh basil. Serve hot.

 Tips
✓ Substitute equal parts cashews for almonds.
✓ I prefer making this recipe with fresh roasted red bell peppers, but you can purchase them jarred in a pinch.

SPINACH ARTICHOKE FLATBREADS

PREP: 5 minutes
COOK: 15 minutes
SERVES: 4

This recipe is for those nights when you wish you had a frozen pizza to pop in the oven. Keeping prepared flatbread in the freezer or pantry is one of my favorite shortcuts for getting a quick, hassle-free meal on the table. And this one is filled with vegetables and can easily be made 100 percent plant-based.

Ingredients

- 4 (8-inch) flatbreads (or naan)
- ½ cup DIY pesto (page 72)
- 1 cup shredded mozzarella cheese (or vegan mozzarella)
- 2 cups baby spinach
- 1 cup marinated artichoke hearts, drained and broken apart
- 1 cup grape tomatoes, halved

Directions

1. Preheat the oven to 425°F.

2. Place the flatbreads on a large baking sheet (or two smaller ones) at least 1 inch apart. Spread each flatbread with pesto evenly from edge to edge (about 2 tablespoons per flatbread). Sprinkle half the mozzarella evenly across the flatbreads.

3. In a large bowl, toss the spinach, artichoke hearts, and tomatoes. Scatter the vegetables on top of the mozzarella. Top flatbreads with the remaining ½ cup mozzarella.

4. Bake 10 to 12 minutes, or until the edges are golden and the cheese is melted.

5. Slice and serve warm.

Love Note

One medium artichoke offers 24 percent of the daily recommended intake of fiber, which is protective against colorectal cancer and cardiovascular disease.

Tips

✓ Frozen spinach works well if thawed and drained. Use a clean cloth napkin or kitchen towel to squeeze all excess liquid from the spinach before adding it to the bowl.
✓ Add black olives or leftover roasted vegetables to this flatbread.

Love Note

More than fresh, canned tomatoes are brimming with lycopene, a compound that's been shown to positively impact blood pressure and help boost heart health.

MUSHROOM AND LENTIL BOLOGNESE

PREP: 15 minutes
COOK: 40 minutes
SERVES: 8

I was the kid at the dinner table who meticulously picked the ground beef from spaghetti and meat sauce. Adult me knows there are other options. Hearty mushrooms and lentils give this sauce a rich flavor that pairs perfectly with pasta—but I'll admit to also wanting to just eat it with a spoon! This "cook once, eat twice" recipe requires a few steps. It's worth the effort, and odds are that you already have most of the ingredients in your pantry.

Ingredients

- 10 ounces mushrooms (recommend shiitake, stems removed)
- 1 medium onion
- 2 carrots, peeled
- ¼ cup olive oil
- 1½ teaspoons salt, divided
- 4 garlic cloves, peeled and minced
- ½ teaspoon red pepper flakes
- 2 tablespoons tomato paste
- 1 (28-ounce) can whole peeled tomatoes, crushed with the back of a spoon
- 2 cups cooked lentils (or one [15-ounce] can, drained and rinsed)
- 1½ cups vegetable broth
- 1 tablespoon reduced-sodium soy sauce
- 1 pound pasta
- ¼ cup sliced fresh basil
- Freshly grated Parmesan cheese

Directions

1. Pulse the mushrooms in a food processor until finely chopped. Remove and set aside. Pulse the onion in the food processor until finely diced. Set aside. Then pulse the carrots until finely diced. Set aside.

2. In a large stockpot, heat the olive oil over medium heat. Add the mushrooms and 1 teaspoon of the salt. Cook about 5 to 7 minutes, until the mushrooms start to brown and the liquid starts to evaporate.

3. Add the onion, carrots, garlic, and red pepper flakes. Cook for about 5 minutes. Add the tomato paste, stirring frequently until it coats the vegetables. Cook for about 2 to 3 minutes more.

4. Add the canned tomatoes, lentils, vegetable broth, and soy sauce. Bring to a boil, then reduce the heat to low. Simmer for at least 20 minutes or until the sauce is thickened. Taste and add salt, if needed.

5. While the sauce simmers, prepare the pasta according to package directions.

6. When the sauce has thickened, ladle half the sauce into a shallow bowl to cool and later freeze. Add the cooked, drained pasta to the remaining sauce in the pot and stir to coat.

7. Portion into four pasta bowls or plates. Top with the basil and freshly grated Parmesan cheese.

Tips

✓ The type of tomatoes and broth you use will significantly impact flavor. Be sure to taste as you cook and adjust the salt accordingly.

✓ This recipe makes 2 quarts of sauce. Serve one with a pound of pasta and freeze one quart for an easy meal on a rainy day.

✓ For an extra layer of flavor, sub ½ cup dry white wine for ½ cup of the vegetable broth.

BLACK BEANS AND CHEESE GRITS

PREP: 5 minutes
COOK: 20 minutes
SERVES: 4

There are two things I always have on hand: grits and black beans. This recipe merges a staple I grew up on (grits) and a bean I was first introduced to when I became a vegan in college. I kept this recipe simple by using canned black beans. Refer to my bean cooking guide (page 61) to make them from dried beans if you prefer. This dish is made with pantry staples that are brightened up with fresh bell pepper and red onion, with optional avocado, green onion, and herbs for garnish.

Ingredients

CHEESE GRITS:
- 4 cups vegetable or chicken broth, plus more if needed
- 1 cup quick-cooking grits or stone-ground grits
- 1 teaspoon salt or to taste
- 2 tablespoons butter (or vegan butter)
- ½ cup shredded cheddar cheese (or vegan cheddar)

SAUCED BLACK BEANS:
- 1 tablespoon avocado or other oil
- ½ cup diced red onion
- 1 cup diced green bell pepper
- ½ teaspoon chili powder
- 2 cups cooked black beans (about one [15-ounce] can, drained and rinsed)
- 1 8-ounce can tomato sauce
- 1 bunch green onions, chopped, for garnish
- 1 avocado, sliced, for garnish
- Cilantro, chopped, for garnish

Directions

1. **Cook the grits.** Bring the broth to a boil in a medium pot. Stir in the grits. Once the grits come to a boil, reduce heat to low. Cover and cook for 15 to 20 minutes (or about 40 minutes for stone-ground grits), stirring frequently with a whisk until the grits are plump, smooth, and creamy. Remove from the heat and stir in the salt, butter, and cheddar.

2. **Make the beans.** While the grits cook, prepare the beans. Heat the oil in a large skillet over medium-high heat. Sauté the onion and bell pepper for about 5 minutes, until soft. Add the chili powder and cook an additional 1 minute, until evenly distributed. Stir in the black beans and tomato sauce. Cook on medium-low heat until everything is heated through and the sauce thickens, about 15 minutes.

3. Spoon the grits into a serving dish. Top with black beans and garnish with green onion, avocado, and cilantro, if using.

Feel like flexing? Add cooked sliced chicken or vegan sausage to the black beans before topping the grits.

Tips

- ✓ Need a shortcut? Swap in a high-quality salsa for the pepper, onion, and tomato sauce. Heat through and serve over the grits.
- ✓ Add more broth or a splash of milk to loosen stiff grits or to reheat them on the stovetop or in the microwave.

CAULIFLOWER AND AVOCADO TACOS

PREP: 10 minutes
COOK: 25 minutes
MAKES: 8 tacos

Taco Tuesday looks a little different this week! While I love a traditional authentic taco, I'm all for getting creative. This recipe takes a California-fresh, veggie-forward approach. These tacos are built with seasoned cauliflower that's been roasted until charred and are topped with a simple, creamy, garlicky avocado mash and crunchy radishes. For a complete meal, serve them with refried or stewed pinto or black beans and salad greens or slaw.

Ingredients

- 2 tablespoons taco seasoning (page 75)
- 2 tablespoons avocado or other oil
- 4 cups bite-size cauliflower florets (about 1 small head)
- 1 medium avocado, peeled and pitted
- ½ lime, juiced, or more to taste
- 2 cloves fresh garlic, peeled and grated
- ⅛ teaspoon salt, or to taste
- 8 (4-inch) soft tortillas (I prefer corn)
- 2 small radishes, thinly sliced
- ¼ cup fresh cilantro, chopped

Directions

1. Preheat the oven to 450°F. Line a baking sheet with parchment paper or spray with oil.

2. **Prep the cauliflower.** Whisk the taco seasoning and oil in a large mixing bowl. Add the cauliflower florets and toss until well coated. Spread the cauliflower on the baking sheet in a single layer. Roast for 20 to 25 minutes, or until the cauliflower is tender and lightly charred.

3. **Make the avocado mash.** In a small bowl, use a fork or the back of a spoon to mash the avocado, lime juice, garlic, and salt until combined.

4. **Warm the tortillas.** Heat the tortillas in a dry skillet over medium to medium-high heat for 30 to 60 seconds per side, or carefully over a flame on the stovetop for 15 to 30 seconds per side, until warm and slightly crispy. Keep warm and pliable by wrapping them in a clean kitchen towel on a plate.

5. **Assemble the tacos.** Evenly layer the avocado mash, cauliflower, and radish slices over the tortillas and sprinkle with the cilantro.

6. Serve warm with seasoned black beans or other beans if desired.

Love Note

I love soft corn tortillas for the bold flavor, and the extra fiber is a bonus. But there are plenty of tasty tortilla options, including almond, jicama, quinoa, chickpea, and cassava–coconut flour tortillas.

Tip ✓ Try swapping in the all-purpose BBQ seasoning (page 75) for the taco seasoning for a sweeter spin on this recipe.

TOMATO, OLIVE, AND ARUGULA FRITTATA

PREP: 5 minutes
COOK: 20 minutes
SERVES: 4

I love making frittatas for dinner. It's the perfect way to use up lots of produce while getting a complete meal on the table in less than 20 minutes. This one also looks good enough to wow a crowd for brunch. The blistered tomatoes add depth and a hint of sweetness, the olives deliver a delectably briny flavor, and the arugula adds a peppery pop of color.

Love Note

Salty and rich, olives are a good source of both monounsaturated fat and vitamin E, a powerful antioxidant.

Tip

✓ Kalamata olives are delicious and easy to find, but any quality black olives work. Just remember to check for pits!

Ingredients

- 6 large eggs
- ¼ cup whole milk or cream
- 2 tablespoons extra-virgin olive oil, plus more for garnish
- 1½ cups grape tomatoes
- 1 teaspoon salt, divided
- ½ small red onion, thinly sliced
- 3 cups arugula (or baby spinach), plus more for garnish
- ¼ teaspoon freshly cracked black pepper
- ¼ cup pitted, chopped kalamata olives, plus more for garnish
- ¼ cup crumbled feta cheese, plus more for garnish

Directions

1. Preheat the oven to 350°F. Whisk the eggs and milk in a medium bowl. Set aside.

2. Heat the olive oil in a 10- or 12-inch oven-safe skillet over medium-high heat. Add the tomatoes, and season with ½ teaspoon of the salt. Cook undisturbed for 1 minute. Continue cooking, turning the tomatoes so they brown on all sides for about 3 minutes. Remove the tomatoes from the pan with a slotted spoon. Set aside.

3. Add the onion and cook for 3 to 5 minutes, until soft but not browned.

4. Add the arugula to the pan and let it wilt for about 30 seconds. Add the tomatoes back to the pan, season all the vegetables with the remaining ½ teaspoon of salt and the pepper. Stir to evenly distribute.

5. Reduce the heat to medium-low. Pour the egg mixture over the vegetables. Sprinkle evenly with olives and feta. Cook for 1 to 2 minutes, until the edges start to set.

6. Transfer the skillet to the oven and bake for 8 to 10 minutes, until the eggs are cooked through—the top will be dry and lightly browned. For more color, place the frittata under the broiler for up to 1 minute.

7. Remove the frittata from the oven and let it cool in the skillet for about 5 minutes, then slide it onto a plate. Top with extra arugula, feta, olives, salt, pepper, and a drizzle of extra-virgin olive oil. Slice and serve warm or at room temperature.

ROSEMARY-ROASTED SALMON AND GRAPES

PREP: 10 minutes
COOK: 10 minutes
SERVES: 4

Equally suitable for a quick weeknight meal or an elegant dinner party, this roasted salmon and grapes recipe is one of my favorite pairings. The grapes get even sweeter as they release their juices for a jammy finish, while aromatic rosemary adds an earthy, savory flavor. The salmon cooks perfectly in the broiler or oven, freeing your hands to set the table for this gorgeous dish.

Ingredients

- 2 cups red or black grapes
- 1 pound salmon, sliced into four 4-ounce fillets
- 2 tablespoons extra-virgin olive oil
- 2 garlic cloves, peeled and grated
- 1 teaspoon kosher salt
- ½ teaspoon freshly cracked black pepper
- 4 sprigs fresh rosemary, leaves only
- 4 cups fresh arugula, baby spinach, baby kale, or other greens

Directions

1. Position an oven rack about 6 to 8 inches from the heat source.

2. Place the grapes and salmon, skin side down, on a baking sheet in an even layer. Coat evenly with the olive oil, garlic, salt, pepper, and rosemary leaves.

3. Broil* on high for about 8 to 10 minutes, until the salmon reaches an internal temperature of 145°F and the grapes are slightly blistered and jammy. Serve on a bed of arugula or other greens, allowing any grape juice to lightly dress the greens.

* Alternative cooking method: Bake at 375°F for 10 to 12 minutes until the salmon reaches an internal temperature of 145°F.

Love Note

Eating a variety of grapes may help maintain healthy blood flow and function.

 Tip ✓ No fresh rosemary? Swap in another hardy herb such as thyme or tarragon.

Love Note

"Lite" coconut milk is simply full-fat coconut milk with water added. Consider buying the full-fat can and adding your own water.

QUICK COCONUT CHICKPEA STEW

PREP: 8 minutes
COOK: 20 minutes
SERVES: 4

Slightly sweet with a lot of spice and completely satisfying, this thick stew is comfort food in a bowl. With its mix of aromatics, warm spices, and hearty vegetables simmered in a rich coconut milk broth, this is a recipe you'll want to make over and over again! I like to serve it with rice or grilled flatbread. You can top this stew with a dash of hot sauce or a cool swirl of yogurt.

Ingredients

- 2 tablespoons coconut oil
- 1 sweet onion, diced
- ½ cup diced red bell pepper
- 3 garlic cloves, peeled and grated
- 1-inch piece fresh ginger, peeled and grated
- ½ teaspoon smoked paprika
- ½ teaspoon ground turmeric powder
- ¼ teaspoon red pepper flakes
- 1 can full-fat coconut milk
- 4 cups bite-size cauliflower florets (1 small head)
- 2 cups cooked chickpeas (or one [15-ounce] can chickpeas, drained and rinsed)
- 1 tablespoon tomato paste
- 1 teaspoon kosher salt
- 6 cups fresh spinach (9 ounces)
- 1 lime, juiced
- Cooked rice, for serving
- Cilantro, for garnish
- Cashews, for garnish

Directions

1. Heat the oil in a large skillet over medium heat. Sauté the onion and bell pepper for 3 to 5 minutes, until the onion is translucent.

2. Add the garlic, ginger, smoked paprika, turmeric, and red pepper flakes. Cook for 1 to 2 minutes, making sure the garlic doesn't burn.

3. Add the coconut milk, cauliflower, chickpeas, tomato paste, and salt. Cook for 10 to 12 minutes, until the cauliflower is fork-tender. Stir in the spinach. Remove from the heat. Add the lime juice.

4. Serve with rice and garnish with cilantro and cashews.

Tips

✓ You can use olive, avocado, or another neutral oil instead of coconut oil.
✓ For more heat, add up to ½ teaspoon red pepper flakes.
✓ Chop or break the cauliflower into pieces that are about the same size for even cooking.
✓ No fresh spinach? Use frozen, thawed spinach, or swap in another quick-cooking leafy green.

WINTER SQUASH RED CURRY

PREP: 10 minutes
COOK: 25 minutes
SERVES: 4

Red lentils are my go-to for quick, protein-packed meals on weeknights. They cook in less than 20 minutes and provide a nice pop of color to any meal. Another colorful addition, butternut squash balances the spices in this rich fall curry with a little sweetness. I usually serve this dish with rice or buttery flatbread.

Love Note

"Squash" comes from the Narragansett Native American word *askutasquash,* which means "eaten raw or uncooked." These fruits are native to the Americas and are quite versatile in the kitchen.

Ingredients

- 2 tablespoons olive oil or other neutral oil
- 1 small onion, diced
- 3 garlic cloves, peeled and minced
- 3 tablespoons red curry paste
- 2 cups cubed butternut squash
- 2 cups vegetable broth
- 1 (15-ounce) can full-fat coconut milk
- 2 tablespoons tomato paste
- 1 cup red lentils, uncooked
- Salt
- Black pepper
- 2 cups baby spinach
- ¼ to ½ cup toasted and salted cashews, chopped (optional)
- Cilantro (optional)

OPTIONAL SERVING IDEAS:
- Rice, roasted cauliflower, or flatbread

Directions

1. Heat the oil in a deep skillet or large pot over medium-high heat. Add the onion and cook for about 2 minutes, just until the onion starts to turn golden. Stir in the garlic and curry paste. Cook for about 1 minute, until the curry paste is fully incorporated.

2. Stir in the butternut squash, broth, coconut milk, tomato paste, and lentils. Cover and cook on medium-low heat for about 12 minutes, stirring occasionally, until the lentils and squash are cooked but not falling apart. Add salt and pepper to taste.

3. Add the spinach, and cook for 3 to 5 minutes, until it wilts into the curry. Serve over rice, cauliflower, or with your favorite flatbread. Top with chopped roasted cashews and cilantro, if using.

Tips
- ✓ In a hurry? Swap the butternut squash for a can of plain pumpkin.
- ✓ As written, this is not a spicy dish. The type of curry paste you use will significantly affect the flavor. Use a mild red curry paste, a spicy chili paste, or a homemade paste you love.

PINTO BEAN CAKES WITH AVOCADO SALSA

PREP: 15 minutes using cooked beans
COOK: 10 minutes
SERVES: 4

I love pinto beans the traditional southern way, simmered low and slow in a big pot and served over rice—usually on a Sunday. These pinto bean cakes are a long way from how I grew up eating them but no less satisfying. This recipe was inspired by the sweet corn cakes I used to get at a popular casual-dining restaurant when I was in college. It was one of the first times I'd ever had avocado, and I fell in love with it. The pinto bean cakes are smooth and creamy inside, with a crispy crust topped with a fresh and flavorful avocado salsa.

Tips
- ✓ Drain the pinto beans over a bowl or large liquid measuring cup to reserve the cooking liquid.
- ✓ The pinto cakes are best served right away but can be reheated in the toaster or a conventional oven.

Ingredients

PINTO CAKES:
- 3½ cups cooked pinto beans (or two 15-ounce cans, no-salt added) drained, with cooking (or can) liquid reserved, and rinsed
- ½ cup fine cornmeal
- ½ cup minced red onion
- 1 teaspoon smoked paprika
- 1 teaspoon garlic powder
- ½ teaspoon salt
- ½ teaspoon black pepper
- ¼ cup olive oil or other neutral oil for frying
- Fresh chopped cilantro, for garnish
- Lime, for garnish

AVOCADO SALSA:
- 1 ripe medium avocado, diced
- 1 medium tomato, diced
- ¼ medium red onion, diced
- 1 garlic clove, peeled and minced
- 1 lime, juiced, plus more for topping
- ¼ cup fresh cilantro, chopped
- Kosher salt to taste

Directions

1. Preheat the oven to a warming temperature, about 170°F.
2. **For the pinto cakes:** In a large bowl, mash the pinto beans, cornmeal, onion, smoked paprika, garlic powder, salt, and pepper using a potato masher or fork. Add 2 to 4 tablespoons of the bean liquid, 1 tablespoon at a time, until the mixture holds together well but is not wet. Divide the mixture into 8 equal portions. Then, using wet hands, shape each portion into a 3-inch patty.
3. Heat 2 tablespoons of the oil in a large skillet over medium-high heat. Add 4 patties to the hot oil. Cook the patties for 2 to 3 minutes on each side until a crisp, golden crust forms. Transfer the patties to a warming rack in the oven. Repeat with the remaining 4 patties.
4. **To make the salsa:** In a medium bowl, gently toss all the ingredients together.
5. **To serve:** Top two patties with ¼ of the salsa mixture. Garnish with cilantro and lime juice.

ONE-SKILLET SPINACH AND MUSHROOM LASAGNA

PREP: 10 minutes
COOK: 50 minutes
SERVES: 6 to 8

The only thing better than a one-pan dish is when someone else volunteers to do the dishes! This one-skillet vegetarian lasagna packs a lot of nutrition and goodness into one pan with only about 10 minutes of hands-on prep time.

Ingredients

- 4 tablespoons extra-virgin olive oil, divided, plus more for garnish
- 1 small onion, diced
- 1 pound button or baby bella mushrooms, sliced
- 2 garlic cloves, peeled and minced
- Pinch of red pepper flakes
- 1 (28-ounce) can whole peeled tomatoes
- ½ teaspoon salt, plus more to taste
- ½ teaspoon dried oregano
- 1½ cups vegetable broth
- 8 ounces lasagna noodles, broken into 2-inch pieces
- 1 cup ricotta, at room temperature
- ¼ cup freshly grated Parmesan cheese
- ¼ cup fresh basil, chopped fine (or 2 teaspoons dry), plus more for garnish
- ¼ teaspoon cracked black pepper, plus more to taste
- 4 cups fresh baby spinach, chopped
- ½ cup shredded mozzarella

Directions

1. Heat 2 tablespoons of the olive oil in a large oven-proof skillet over medium-high heat. Add the onion and cook until it starts to soften, about 5 minutes. Add the mushrooms and season with a big pinch of salt and pepper. Sauté until tender, about 5 to 7 minutes.

2. Make space in the middle of the skillet. Add the remaining 2 tablespoons of olive oil. Add the garlic and red pepper flakes. Cook for about 30 seconds—just until fragrant. Don't allow the garlic to brown.

3. Pour in the tomatoes. Use a wooden spoon to release any brown bits from the bottom of the pan and to crush the tomatoes. Add the salt and the oregano.

4. Reduce the heat to medium and simmer for at least 20 to 25 minutes, stirring occasionally, until the sauce starts to thicken. Pour the broth into the sauce. Nestle the lasagna noodles into the skillet, making sure they are fully covered by the liquid. Simmer uncovered for about 20 minutes, stirring occasionally, until the pasta is just tender. (If needed, add up to ¼ cup of broth at a time to keep the pasta immersed.)

5. While the pasta cooks, make the herbed ricotta. In a small bowl, mix the ricotta, Parmesan, basil, and black pepper until combined.

6. During the last 5 minutes the pasta is cooking, stir in the spinach, then scatter large spoonfuls of the herbed ricotta mixture over the lasagna. Sprinkle with the mozzarella. Remove from the heat. Cover and let sit for 5 minutes, until the cheese melts. Optional: Broil 3 to 4 minutes to brown the cheese.

7. Serve warm garnished with fresh basil and olive oil if desired.

SPINACH AND RICOTTA LINGUINE

PREP: 10 minutes
COOK: 20 minutes
SERVES: 4

Vegetable sauces are an easy way to incorporate more nutrition into any meal—especially pasta. This garlicky, creamy spinach sauce gives pesto-meets-Alfredo vibes. The dollops of ricotta, toasted walnuts, and olive oil deliver an elegant, restaurant-worthy finish packed with flavor. Spinach is at its best in the spring, but this simple dish can be served at any time of the year.

Love Note

Spinach is rich in carotenoids, and eating it with a fat like olive oil helps you absorb more of those powerful immune boosters!

Tips

✓ Add cooked white beans, chicken, or salmon for more protein.
✓ Serve this dish soon after blending the sauce. As it sits, the spinach sauce will start to oxidize and the bright green color will start to brown.

Ingredients

- 1 pound linguine
- 3 garlic cloves, peeled and smashed
- ¼ to ½ teaspoon red pepper flakes (depending on heat preference)
- 2 tablespoons extra-virgin olive oil, plus more for topping
- 1 pound fresh spinach
- 2 tablespoons broth (choose your favorite)
- ½ lemon, zested and juiced
- ⅓ cup ricotta cheese (or vegan ricotta), plus more for topping
- ½ teaspoon salt
- ¼ teaspoon freshly cracked black pepper, plus more for topping
- ¼ cup toasted walnuts

Directions

1. Cook the linguine according to package directions. Before draining, reserve ½ cup of the pasta water.

2. In a large skillet, sauté the garlic and red pepper flakes in the olive oil over medium heat for 1 to 2 minutes, until fragrant but not brown.

3. Add the spinach and broth. Cover and cook on medium heat for 3 to 5 minutes, until the spinach wilts.

4. Transfer the mixture, including all the liquid remaining in the skillet, to a heat-safe blender. Add ¼ cup of the reserved pasta water, the lemon juice, ricotta, salt, and black pepper. Blend until smooth and creamy, adding more reserved pasta water, 1 tablespoon at a time, if needed to reach desired texture.

5. Add the sauce back to the skillet and heat over medium, stirring frequently, until hot. Add the hot pasta and lemon zest (reserving ¼ to ½ teaspoon for topping). Toss to coat.

6. Serve warm topped with dollops of ricotta, toasted walnuts, the reserved lemon zest, a drizzle of olive oil, and freshly cracked black pepper.

Make it vegan: Swap vegan ricotta and vegetable broth. Because almond ricotta tends to have a drier texture, you may need to add more pasta water to achieve a smooth sauce.

BLACK BEAN-STUFFED SWEET PLANTAINS

PREP: 10 minutes
COOK: 30 minutes
SERVES: 4

Canoas are a traditional Puerto Rican preparation of plantains stuffed with a savory ground-beef filling. This recipe offers a vegetarian spin using black beans seasoned with onions, peppers, and garlic. It's sweet with a little heat. Add the cheese—vegan or regular—to help round out the flavors.

Love Note

Plantains are rich in phenolic compounds, which function as antioxidants, reduce inflammation, and can optimize gut health.

Tips

✓ Use firm, ripe plantains that have some black speckling but are not fully black for this recipe.

✓ Buy your plantains a few days before you're ready to make this recipe. They will continue to ripen on your kitchen counter.

Ingredients

- 2 large ripe plantains
- 2 tablespoons extra-virgin olive oil
- ½ medium red or sweet onion, diced
- 1 medium red or green bell pepper, diced
- 1 medium jalapeño, seeded and minced (remove ribs for less heat)
- 3 garlic cloves, peeled and minced
- ½ teaspoon ground cumin
- 1 tablespoon tomato paste
- ¼ cup broth or water
- ½ teaspoon salt
- 2 cups cooked black beans (or one [15-ounce] can unseasoned black beans, drained and rinsed)
- ¼ cup queso fresco (or vegan queso fresco)
- Blender salsa (page 71)

Directions

1. Preheat the oven to 400°F. Spray a rimmed baking sheet with olive oil or line with parchment paper.

2. Cut off the ends of the plantains and remove the peels.

3. Place the plantains on the prepared baking sheet. Spray them lightly with oil. Bake for 15 minutes. Flip and bake for 15 minutes more. The plantains should be golden and tender but not soft.

4. Heat the olive oil in a large skillet over medium-high heat. Sauté the onion, bell pepper, and jalapeño until the onion is translucent, about 5 to 7 minutes. Add the garlic and cumin. Cook for about 1 minute, stirring frequently, until the cumin is fragrant.

5. Reduce the heat to medium. Add the tomato paste, broth or water, salt, and black beans. Cook for about 5 minutes, until the beans are heated through and most of the liquid has evaporated.

6. Remove the plantains from the oven. When cool enough to handle, slice ¾ of the way down the center curved side of each plantain, leaving 1 inch on each end. Pull the plantains open using the back of a spoon, and press the bottoms and sides to create a well.

7. Spoon the filling evenly into the plantains. Top evenly with the queso fresco. Bake for about 5 to 7 minutes. Serve warm with the fresh salsa.

RED RICE

PREP: 5 minutes
COOK: 45 minutes
SERVES: 8

Visit low country South Carolina and you're bound to see red rice and/ or perloo (a rice dish typically made with shellfish, vegetables, and pork) simmering away in many kitchens. Rice is a Carolina staple. When I was growing up, we always had rice on the table, and we still do. This Gullah-inspired red rice recipe gets its rich color from tomato paste and is traditionally made with bacon or pork sausage and a pinch of sugar for balance. Adding a little extra plant-based or regular sausage takes this typical side dish to main status.

Love Note

White rice is comfort food for many and is an easy-to-digest source of energy. And enriched white rice is a good source of manganese, iron, thiamine, and folate.

Ingredients

- 2 cups parboiled long grain rice
- 3 tablespoons olive oil or other neutral oil
- 1 large sweet onion, diced
- 1 large green bell pepper, diced
- 12 ounces smoked sausage (or vegan smoked sausage), diced
- 8 ounces tomato paste
- 2 garlic cloves, peeled and minced
- 1 teaspoon sugar
- 2 teaspoons salt
- 1 teaspoon black pepper
- Pinch of cayenne pepper or dash of hot sauce
- 2 cups water
- Chopped fresh parsley, for garnish

Directions

1. Preheat the oven to 350°F.
2. Rinse the rice until the water runs clear. Drain and set aside.
3. Heat the oil in a large (12-inch) oven-safe skillet with a lid or shallow Dutch oven over medium-high heat. Sauté the onion, bell pepper, and sausage in the oil for 5 to 8 minutes, stirring occasionally, until the onion and pepper soften and the sausage starts to brown.
4. Add the tomato paste, garlic, sugar, salt, black pepper, and cayenne pepper or hot sauce. Cook until fragrant, about 1 minute. Add the rice. Stir, toasting the rice for 2 to 3 minutes. Don't allow it to brown. Add the water (it should just cover the rice) and cover with a tight-fitting lid.
5. Transfer to the oven and bake for about 30 minutes, until the liquid is fully absorbed and the rice is tender. Fluff the cooked rice with a fork. Garnish with the parsley.

Change it up: Add sautéed shrimp or your favorite protein to the cooked rice.

Tips

- ✓ Use your favorite chicken or vegetable broth instead of water for more flavor, but be sure to reduce the salt to account for the sodium in the broth.
- ✓ Equipment matters here: I use a shallow Dutch oven (a 3.6-quart enameled cast-iron covered casserole), which is great at conducting heat. A thinner skillet may have a different cook time.
- ✓ If you don't have a Dutch oven or an oven-safe skillet with a lid, follow the steps through toasting the rice. Add the water to your skillet, then transfer everything to a 9-by-13-inch baking dish coated with cooking spray, cover tightly with foil, and bake as is.

SPICY BBQ TOFU LETTUCE CUPS

PREP: 30 minutes
COOK: 20 minutes
SERVES: about 4

The first time I had tofu was when I was vegan in college. I'll admit, it was not my favorite—but I did find a restaurant that made the best barbecue tofu. In developing a tofu recipe for this book, I decided to honor my first experience by pairing tofu with a tangy, vinegary Carolina-style barbecue sauce. This simple tofu recipe—a food processor does most of the work for you—is versatile. Serve it in lettuce cups or dress it up in a bowl.

Ingredients

TOFU:
- 14 ounces extra-firm tofu
- 2 medium carrots, peeled and coarsely chopped, plus more for garnish
- 1 medium red or green bell pepper, coarsely chopped
- 1 medium red onion, coarsely chopped
- 1 jalapeño, halved and seeded
- 2 garlic cloves, peeled
- 2 tablespoons neutral oil
- Salt
- Black pepper

BARBECUE SAUCE:
- ½ cup apple cider vinegar
- ⅓ cup ketchup
- 2 tablespoons dark brown sugar
- 1 tablespoon Worcestershire sauce (regular or vegan)
- 1 teaspoon mustard powder
- Dash of hot sauce (or pinch of cayenne pepper)
- ½ teaspoon salt
- ¼ teaspoon black pepper

LETTUCE CUPS:
- 1 head butter or other lettuce, leaves separated
- 2 green onions, chopped, for garnish
- Cooked rice, for serving

Directions

1. Drain the tofu then wrap it in a clean, lint-free kitchen towel. Put it between two plates and place a heavy object, such as a cast-iron skillet, on top to press out the excess liquid. Press for at least 30 minutes, then pat the tofu dry.

2. In a food processor, pulse the carrot, bell pepper, onion, jalapeño, and garlic until finely chopped, about 8 to 10 pulses.

3. Tear the tofu and add it to the food processor. Pulse 3 or 4 times, until coarsely chopped.

4. Heat the oil in a large skillet over medium-high heat. Add the pulsed vegetable and tofu to the skillet. Season with the salt and pepper to taste. Sauté, stirring occasionally, until the tofu starts to brown and most liquid evaporates, about 10 minutes.

5. While the vegetables cook, whisk all the sauce ingredients in a small bowl. Pour the sauce over the vegetable-tofu mixture. Cook over medium heat until the mixture has thickened, about 5 to 7 minutes.

6. Spoon the BBQ tofu and cooked rice into the lettuce cups. Garnish with the green onion and carrots.

Tips

- ✓ If desired, remove the jalapeño ribs to reduce the spiciness.
- ✓ Swap in your favorite store-bought barbecue sauce to make this meal in even less time.
- ✓ Want a little more? Swap the lettuce cups for your favorite wrap, or make a BBQ tofu bowl with rice and extra crunchy vegetables.
- ✓ Beware of pepper hands. Use gloves when slicing into jalapeños or other hot peppers to prevent their capsaicin oil from getting on your skin or in your eyes.

Love Note

Are you Team Cilantro? This little green herb can divide a room, thanks to a gene that makes some people strongly dislike cilantro.

SHEET PAN FAJITAS

PREP: 10 minutes
COOK: 25 minutes
SERVES: 4

I immediately fall in love with any meal that can be made entirely on a sheet pan, and this one is no different. Choose your own adventure: Make these sheet pan fajitas with fish or mushrooms—or both! Homemade taco seasoning sprinkled over bell peppers, red onion, and your choice of meaty portobello mushrooms or your favorite fish makes for a mostly hands-off dinner that everyone will love. Serve with your favorite toppings and warm tortillas or lettuce wraps for fajita night.

Ingredients

- 2 medium red bell peppers, sliced in ½- or ¼-inch-thick strips
- 1 large green bell pepper, sliced in ½- or ¼-inch-thick strips
- 1 medium red onion, sliced
- 2 tablespoons olive oil or avocado oil, divided
- 2 tablespoons taco seasoning (page 75), divided
- 1 pound cod, sliced into 4-ounce fillets (or 1 pound portobello mushrooms, cut into ½- to ¾-inch pieces)
- 1 lime, juiced
- 8 warm soft tortillas or lettuce leaves
- ¼ cup chopped fresh cilantro (optional)
- Avocado (optional)
- Salsa (optional)
- Sour cream (optional)

Directions

1. Preheat the oven to 400°F. Line a sheet pan with parchment paper.

2. Arrange the red and green bell peppers and onions on the sheet pan in a single layer. Drizzle with 1 tablespoon of the oil and 1 tablespoon of the taco seasoning. Roast in the oven for 10 minutes.

3. Meanwhile, pat the cod (or mushrooms) dry to remove any excess water. In a medium bowl, coat the cod (or mushrooms) with the remaining 1 tablespoon of oil and 1 tablespoon of taco seasoning. Remove the sheet pan from the oven and move the peppers and onions to the side of the pan to make room for the fish (or mushrooms). Carefully place the fish (or mushrooms) directly on the pan.

4. Roast in the oven for about 10 more minutes, until the cod reaches an internal temperature of 145°F (or the mushrooms are fork-tender). Squeeze the lime juice over the cooked fajitas.

5. Serve the fajitas with the tortillas or lettuce leaves, and top with the cilantro, avocado, salsa, and sour cream if desired.

Tips
- ✓ Swap in any skinless, thick white fish or salmon for the cod.
- ✓ Store leftover fajitas in a sealed container in the refrigerator for 2 days (with fish) or 3 to 5 days (with vegetables only). Serve with fresh tortillas or use to top a grain bowl.

KALE SLAW WITH PEANUT DRESSING

PREP: 15 minutes
COOK: 0 minutes
SERVES: 8

Kale is the poster child of eating well for good reason: Just one cup delivers more vitamin C than an orange, and it's a good source of many other vitamins, minerals, and antioxidants too. In this simple salad, humble kale gets a nutty upgrade with a peanut dressing and carrots. Though any type of kale will work, I like using dinosaur, also known as Tuscan or lacinato, versus curly kale for a more tender salad.

Ingredients

- ½ cup avocado, olive, or peanut oil
- ¼ cup apple cider vinegar
- 2 tablespoons smooth, natural peanut butter, at room temperature
- 1 teaspoon light brown sugar or date sugar
- Pinch of coarse salt
- 2 bunches of kale, julienned
- 1 cup shredded carrots, plus more for garnish
- ½ cup chopped lightly salted and roasted peanuts, plus more for garnish

Directions

1. In a small bowl, whisk the oil, vinegar, peanut butter, sugar, and salt until smooth and creamy.

2. Place the kale in a large mixing bowl. Add the dressing and, with clean hands, massage it into the kale for 3 to 5 minutes by gently kneading the dressing into the leaves. You'll know it's ready when the kale leaves start to loosen and take on a silky, darker green color.

3. Add the carrots and peanuts and toss until combined. Top with extra peanuts and carrots.

Love Note

Massaging a bit of oil or dressing into raw kale helps break down the fibers in the greens, making the salad easier to chew and more enjoyable to eat.

Tips
- ✓ Drippy, natural peanut butter is my go-to for making dressings and sauces. If yours is more stiff, heat it for a few seconds in the microwave to loosen before whisking it with the other dressing ingredients.
- ✓ This salad is perfect atop tempeh or fish tacos, in a wrap with edamame or white beans, or alongside your favorite barbecued protein or crispy tofu for dinner.
- ✓ Kale is a hardy green, so this slaw is perfect for make-ahead lunches and meal prep.

SOCCA WITH SAUTÉED VEGETABLES

PREP: 5 minutes
COOK: 15 minutes
SERVES: 4

Socca is a French flatbread made from chickpea flour, water, and olive oil. When I first tried it, I was amazed at how easy it was to make something that tastes so good. It reminds me of corn bread but is much simpler to prepare and packed with protein and fiber. I like to have it with salt and herbs as a snack or appetizer, but adding sautéed or roasted vegetables turns this recipe into a full meal. If you're not already stocking chickpea flour, you will be after making this!

Love Note

Chickpea flour is incredibly satiating and nutrient rich, providing several vitamins and minerals and a day's worth of folate in one cup.

Ingredients

SOCCA:

- 1 cup chickpea flour
- ½ teaspoon kosher salt
- ½ teaspoon garlic powder
- 1 cup warm water
- 1½ tablespoons extra-virgin olive oil, plus more for coating pan

SAUTÉED VEGETABLES:

- 1 tablespoon extra-virgin olive oil
- 2 cups kale or other greens
- 10 ounces mushrooms, thickly sliced
- 2 garlic cloves, peeled and minced
- 1 cup grape tomatoes, halved
- 1 teaspoon coarse salt
- ½ teaspoon freshly cracked black pepper

Directions

1. Place a well-seasoned cast-iron skillet in the oven and preheat the oven to 450°F.

2. **Make the socca.** Whisk the flour, salt, and garlic powder in a medium bowl to combine. Whisk in the water and olive oil until the mixture is smooth and the liquid is incorporated. Let it sit while the oven preheats.

3. Once the oven reaches 450°F, remove the skillet and spray or brush it generously with olive oil. Pour in the batter. Bake for 15 minutes.

4. **Make the sautéed vegetables.** While the socca bakes, heat a large skillet over medium heat with the olive oil. Sauté the kale, mushrooms, and garlic for about 5 minutes, or until desired tenderness. Add the tomatoes. Season with salt and pepper.

5. Serve the vegetables alongside or on top of the warm socca.

Tips

✓ Look for chickpea or garbanzo flour in the flour section of the supermarket or order it online. The ingredient list should simply read "chickpea flour."
✓ Using a very hot skillet creates a lovely crust and allows for maximum flavor.
✓ Experiment with different vegetables. This recipe is the perfect way to clear out extra vegetables from the fridge.
✓ Try socca sprinkled with za'atar, a Middle Eastern herb blend that usually contains salt, sumac, thyme, and/or oregano, and toasted sesame seeds, among other herbs.

ROASTED SHRIMP, PINEAPPLE, AND PEPPER TACOS

PREP: 15 minutes
COOK: 12 minutes
SERVES: 4

These bright and flavorful tacos are a sweet and spicy way to transition to a plant-forward way of eating. I love adding fruit where you might not expect it: Roasted pineapple lends a smoky and sweet juicy flavor to the shrimp, which is balanced by the jalapeño peppers. While those are cooking on the sheet pan, your hands are free to prep your tortillas and a simple sauce that pulls it all together.

Ingredients

TACOS:
- 1 pound medium shrimp, raw, thawed, peeled, and deveined
- 2 tablespoons avocado or olive oil, divided
- 2 teaspoons chili powder
- 2 garlic cloves, peeled and grated
- 1 lime, juiced
- 2 cups fresh sweet pineapple, cut into ¼-inch cubes
- ½ small red onion, sliced into thin wedges
- 1 jalapeño, seeded and sliced into thick strips
- 8 corn or soft taco tortillas

LIME RANCH SAUCE:
- ½ cup Greek yogurt (or vegan mayo)
- ¼ cup chopped fresh cilantro
- 2 garlic cloves, peeled and grated
- ½ teaspoon onion powder
- ½ lime, juiced
- ½ teaspoon salt

Directions

1. Preheat the oven to 425°F. Position one rack in the center of the oven and another near the top for broiling.

2. Toss the shrimp, 1 tablespoon of the oil, the chili powder, garlic, and lime juice in a medium bowl.

3. On a large sheet pan, toss the pineapple, onion, and jalapeño in the remaining 1 tablespoon of oil. Spread in a single layer, ensuring the jalapeño goes cut side down. Add the seasoned shrimp (using tongs to avoid adding extra liquid to the pan). Take care not to crowd the pan.

4. Roast in the oven until the shrimp is cooked through, about 8 to 10 minutes. Move the sheet pan to the top rack. Set the oven to broil on high. Broil for 1 to 2 minutes, allowing everything to turn golden brown.

5. Whisk all the sauce ingredients in a small bowl. Set aside.

6. Heat the tortillas in a dry skillet for 30 to 60 seconds per side over medium to medium-high heat, or carefully over a flame on the stovetop for 15 to 30 seconds per side, until warm and slightly crispy.

7. Evenly portion the shrimp, pineapple, onion, and jalapeño on the warm tortillas. Drizzle with the sauce and serve.

Tip
✓ Roasting the shrimp helps sweeten the tacos. To get a nice char, be sure to dry the shrimp well and leave enough space between each piece on the sheet pan.

LENTIL-STUFFED PEPPERS

PREP: 15 minutes
COOK: 30 minutes
SERVES: 4

Swapping lentils for ground meat gives these traditional stuffed peppers a fiber-rich, plant-forward makeover with a lot of the same flavors. With a little prep, this recipe is mostly hands-off for an easy weeknight meal to feed a crowd. I like to stuff the peppers the night before, refrigerate, then pop the dish in the oven for an easy dinner the next day. It's a filling family meal that's ready in 30 minutes.

Ingredients

- 4 large bell peppers, halved and seeded
- 2 tablespoons extra-virgin olive oil
- 1 small onion, diced
- 2 garlic cloves, peeled and minced
- 1 teaspoon dried oregano
- 2 cups cooked rice
- 2 cups cooked brown or green lentils* (or 1 [15-ounce] can lentils, drained and rinsed)
- 1 (15-ounce) can fire-roasted diced tomatoes, drained
- 1 lemon, juiced
- 1 teaspoon coarse salt
- ½ teaspoon freshly cracked black pepper
- ¼ cup fresh parsley, plus more for garnish
- ½ cup (2 ounces) crumbled feta cheese (or vegan feta)

Directions

1. Preheat the oven to 400°F.

2. Arrange the halved peppers, cut side up, in an oiled 9-by-13-inch baking dish. Season with salt and pepper. Set aside.

3. In a large skillet, sauté the onion in the olive oil over medium heat for about 5 minutes. Stir in the garlic and oregano and cook for 2 to 3 minutes until fragrant. Remove from the heat.

4. Stir in the cooked rice and lentils, tomatoes, lemon juice, salt, pepper, and parsley.

5. Heap the lentil mixture into the halved peppers. Top evenly with crumbled feta.

6. Bake for 30 minutes or until the feta starts to brown. Top with extra parsley and serve.

* Cook your own lentils. Remove any debris and rinse the lentils under running water. Using a large stockpot, bring 1 cup of lentils in 3 cups of water or stock to a boil. Cover. Reduce heat to a simmer. Cook for 15 to 20 minutes, until the lentils are tender. Season with salt and pepper. Drain the excess liquid before adding to the mix.

Tips

- ✓ Swap the rice for another cooked grain such as quinoa, millet, fonio, or cracked bulgur wheat.
- ✓ Know your lentils. If you use canned lentils, adjust the salt to your taste. Use green, brown, or black lentils to maintain a firm texture.
- ✓ Don't have parsley? Swap in an equal amount of fresh basil or try 1½ tablespoons dried parsley or Italian seasoning.

VEGGIE-RICH
SIDES

CRISPY OKRA

PREP: 5 minutes
COOK: 12 minutes
SERVES: 4

This polarizing pod is one of my favorite foods. If you've written off okra because of the "slime factor," try this recipe and take comfort in knowing that you're giving it your best shot. I grew up eating okra with tomatoes, added to soup, simply stewed in a pan, and, of course, fried. Now I usually roast fresh okra because it's so easy, and I love how it gets all crispy and sweet in the oven. I'm confident you'll love it too.

Ingredients

- 1 pound fresh okra
- 1 tablespoon sesame or other oil
- 1 teaspoon red pepper flakes
- Coarse salt, to taste

Directions

1. Preheat the oven to 425°F.

2. Wash and dry the okra. Slice off the tops and cut the okra in half lengthwise.

3. Place the cut okra onto a baking sheet, leaving plenty of space between each piece. Drizzle it with the sesame oil. Sprinkle it with the red pepper flakes and salt to taste.

4. Roast the okra for 10 to 12 minutes, turning it once midway through baking. Remove it from the oven and enjoy as a warm side dish or snack.

Love Note

Okra is an excellent source of vitamin C and a good source of magnesium, folate, and soluble fiber, which helps reduce blood cholesterol and the risk of heart disease.

Tip
✓ Okra is in season from May to October, but you can find frozen okra at most major supermarkets (though frozen won't work in this recipe). Choose small fresh okra pods (about the length of a finger); these are the most flavorful and tender. Long okra pods are tough and fibrous.

HONEY PEPPER BROCCOLI

PREP: 10 minutes
COOK: 25 minutes
SERVES: 4

Broccoli is one of the most popular vegetables in the United States—and that's a good thing, since it's rich in immune-supporting vitamin C. This sweet and tangy glazed version pairs well with fish or can be tossed into a noodle or grain bowl.

Love Note

Broccoli is rich in bioactive compounds such as sulforaphane, which may help reduce the risk of prostate, breast, and colon cancer.

Ingredients

- 1 pound broccoli, cut into florets (stalk removed)
- ¼ cup olive oil
- ¾ teaspoon salt, divided
- ¾ teaspoon pepper, divided
- ¼ cup honey
- ⅓ cup red wine vinegar
- 2 tablespoons butter (or vegan butter)

Directions

1. Place a baking sheet on the bottom rack of the oven. Preheat to 450°F.

2. In a large bowl, toss the broccoli florets in the olive oil and season with ¼ teaspoon each of the salt and the pepper.

3. Remove the hot baking sheet from the oven. Place the broccoli onto the baking sheet, leaving space between the florets to allow the broccoli to roast. Roast on the bottom rack for about 15 minutes, until the broccoli is tender and caramelized on the pan side.

4. While the broccoli roasts, heat the honey in a small saucepan over medium-high heat. Once the honey starts to simmer, reduce the heat to medium-low and continue stirring constantly until the honey becomes lightly browned, about 3 to 4 minutes.

5. Remove the pan from the heat and whisk in the vinegar. Return to medium heat. Whisk in the butter, ½ teaspoon salt, and ½ teaspoon pepper. Cook, whisking constantly, for 3 to 4 minutes, until the sauce takes on a shiny appearance and is slightly thickened into a glaze.

6. Put the roasted broccoli back in the large bowl. Pour the glaze over the broccoli and toss to coat. Serve warm.

Tips
- ✓ Allow the broccoli to breathe. Leaving plenty of space between the florets allows the broccoli to caramelize, not steam. Like other cruciferous vegetables, cooked broccoli doesn't keep long in the refrigerator, so try to eat it within a day or two.
- ✓ Store fresh broccoli unwashed in the refrigerator crisper, wrapped in a damp paper towel, or with the stalk end submerged in water like a bouquet of flowers to help it stay fresh longer.

CHARD WITH TAHINI

PREP: 5 minutes
COOK: 20 minutes
SERVES: 4

This side is kind of like creamed spinach, but nuttier. The tahini and lemon add a satisfying savory flavor that is perfect served with white beans and warm flatbread. If you haven't tried chard, it's usually right next to the spinach in the produce aisle and has a similar mild flavor. It can be enjoyed cooked or raw and prepared much like you'd use spinach.

Ingredients

- 1 bunch chard, rainbow or Swiss
- 2 tablespoons extra-virgin olive oil
- ½ small sweet onion, diced
- 1 to 2 tablespoons water or broth
- 2 tablespoons tahini, at room temperature
- 1 tablespoon fresh lemon juice (about ¼ medium lemon)
- ¼ teaspoon black pepper
- ¼ teaspoon salt if needed

Directions

1. Wash the chard well. Remove the stems and dice them small. Stack and roll the chard leaves and slice them into 1-inch strips.

2. In a large skillet, heat the olive oil over medium-high heat. Add the diced chard stems and the onion. Sauté until tender, about 5 to 7 minutes, stirring frequently.

3. Add the chard leaves and 1 tablespoon of water to the skillet. Reduce the heat to medium-low. Cover and cook for 8 to 10 minutes, just until the chard is tender.

4. While the chard is cooking, in a small bowl, whisk the tahini, lemon juice, pepper, and salt, to taste, until smooth.

5. Stir the tahini mixture into the chard and cook about 2 minutes, until the greens are evenly coated and the sauce is heated through. Remove from the heat and serve immediately.

Love Note

One cup of cooked nutrient-dense chard exceeds your daily needs for vitamin K, which is necessary for bone health and blood clotting.

Tips
- ✓ Don't have chard? Try spinach or kale.
- ✓ Don't overcook the greens. Adjust the cooking time based on how large you slice the chard. Thinner slices will require less braising time.
- ✓ Chard can taste quite salty compared with other greens. Don't add salt until you've tasted the final dish.

NUTTY ROASTED CAULIFLOWER AND GRAPES

PREP: 10 minutes
COOK: 25 minutes
MAKES: about 4 cups

File this recipe under "Don't knock it till you try it." This side dish is a great way to switch things up with a flavor combination that is sweet, nutty, savory, and incredibly satisfying. Both red and black grapes complement the cauliflower with a fruity flavor and a bright pop of color. Finish with toasted almonds, pistachios, or pecans for crunch and a dose of good fats. With fruit, vegetables, and nuts, you can enjoy this one solo, add a scoop to a grain bowl, or have it alongside fish for dinner.

Ingredients

- 6 cups bite-size cauliflower florets (about 1 medium head)
- 1½ cups red or black seedless grapes
- 2 garlic cloves, peeled and minced
- 2 tablespoons extra-virgin olive oil
- ½ teaspoon salt
- ¼ teaspoon cracked black pepper
- ½ cup sliced toasted almonds
- 2 tablespoons grated Parmesan cheese (or vegan Parmesan)
- 2 tablespoons fresh basil, julienned

Directions

1. Preheat the oven to 425°F.

2. Toss the cauliflower, grapes, and garlic with the olive oil on a large baking sheet. Sprinkle evenly with salt and pepper. Spread and space the cauliflower and grapes well on the baking sheet to avoid crowding the pan.

3. Roast in the oven for 20 to 25 minutes, until tender and caramelized. Stir once midway.

4. Remove from the oven. Stir in the almonds and top with the Parmesan and basil. Serve warm.

Love Note

Cauliflower is a versatile vegetable that can stand up to all kinds of flavors. Try it with bold spices, and experiment with different cooking methods, from grilling to pan-roasting to blending it into a silky soup or sauce.

 Tip ✓ Be sure to break the florets into similarly sized pieces to ensure even cooking.

COCONUT-BRAISED COLLARD GREENS

PREP: 15 minutes
COOK: 30 to 45 minutes
SERVES: 4

Collard greens are my ultimate comfort food. I've been eating collards since I was too young to know what they were and had no idea how good this leafy green is for us. Picking, cleaning, cutting, and cooking greens is a labor of love that's worth every single second. While these are not the greens I grew up on, they're just as delicious. With its rich, flavorful broth, this is one of the ways I enjoy eating collard greens and serving them to people who don't eat meat.

Ingredients

- 1 tablespoon olive oil
- 2 garlic cloves, peeled and grated
- 2 teaspoons grated fresh ginger
- ¼ teaspoon red pepper flakes
- 1 small bunch collard greens, cleaned and thinly sliced (about 6 cups)
- ½ cup vegetable broth
- ½ cup canned full-fat coconut milk
- ¼ to ½ teaspoon salt

Directions

1. Heat the olive oil in a large sauté pan over medium heat. Sauté the garlic, ginger and red pepper flakes until fragrant, about 1 minute.

2. Add the collard greens, broth, and coconut milk. Bring to a boil, then lower to a simmer and cover. Cook for 30 to 45 minutes, to the desired tenderness.

3. Serve warm.

Love Note

Cooked collard greens are an excellent source of calcium and vitamin K– two nutrients essential for bone health.

Tips

✓ Collard greens can be a bit bitter. Add a pinch of sugar to reduce the bitterness if desired.
✓ Thicker-cut greens take longer to cook, so adjust the time accordingly.
✓ Adjust the salt based on the saltiness of the broth you use.
✓ Store leftovers in the refrigerator for 1 to 2 days.
✓ Though I am all for convenience, I do not recommend using bagged collard greens, as they can be dry and tend to contain lots of tough stems.

LEMON-WALNUT ROASTED ASPARAGUS

PREP: **10 minutes**
COOK: **8 minutes**
SERVES: **4**

Asparagus and lemon are a classic pair that I've elevated by adding crunchy, heart-healthy walnuts. Asparagus is in season in spring, when it's plentiful and most affordable. For this recipe, I look for thick stalks that can hold up to roasting. When adding raw asparagus to a salad or doing a quick pan sauté, look for thinner stalks that will cook quickly and keep a lovely green color.

Ingredients

- 1 bunch asparagus, trimmed
- 3 tablespoons extra-virgin oil, divided
- ½ teaspoon coarse salt, divided
- ¼ teaspoon fresh cracked black pepper, divided
- 1 lemon, zested and juiced (2 tablespoons juice and 1 teaspoon zest)
- ¼ cup chopped toasted walnuts
- 3 tablespoons diced shallot (1 small)

Directions

1. Preheat the oven to 450°F.

2. Rinse the asparagus and pat it dry. Spread the asparagus in a single layer on a baking sheet. Toss with 1 tablespoon of the olive oil, ¼ teaspoon of the salt, and ⅛ teaspoon of the pepper. Roast for 8 minutes.

3. Meanwhile, in a small bowl, whisk together the remaining 2 tablespoons of olive oil with the lemon juice, and add the walnuts, shallot, and the remaining ¼ teaspoon of salt and ⅛ teaspoon of pepper.

4. Pour the dressing evenly over the cooked asparagus. Sprinkle with the lemon zest and serve.

Love Note

Asparagus shoots are rich in chromium, a trace mineral that has been shown to improve insulin sensitivity.

Tips
✓ Remember that asparagus can be eaten raw—roasting is optional but helps develop flavor and create a more tender bite.
✓ Don't have a shallot? Try a grated sweet onion or top with chives for a mild onion flavor.

SIMPLE ROASTED CABBAGE

PREP: 5 minutes
COOK: 25 minutes
SERVES: 6 to 8

If you haven't roasted cabbage, you are missing out on one of the most flavorful ways to enjoy this oft-forgotten vegetable. I still love the braised cabbage I grew up eating, but roasting creates a new flavor profile by caramelizing the cabbage in a hot pan for a sweet, tender finish. I've offered some simple ways to add more flavor to this already tasty (yet simple) recipe!

Love Note

The humble green cabbage is a good source of plant sterols, which have been shown to help lower LDL, or "bad," cholesterol levels.

Ingredients

- 3 tablespoons extra-virgin olive oil, divided
- 1 medium head green cabbage
- 1 teaspoon coarse salt
- ½ teaspoon black pepper

Directions

1. Preheat the oven to 450°F. Brush a large sheet pan with 1 tablespoon of the olive oil or line it with parchment paper.

2. Cut the head of cabbage in half and remove the core. Slice each half into even wedges—about 6 to 8 wedges, 1 inch thick. Place the wedges on the pan in a single layer. Brush evenly with the remaining 2 tablespoons olive oil and the salt and pepper.

3. Roast the wedges for about 15 minutes, or until golden on the bottom. Use tongs to turn each wedge, taking care to keep it intact. Roast for an additional 10 minutes, until the cabbage is tender but not too soft.

4. Serve warm or at room temperature.

VARIATIONS:
- Try this recipe with red cabbage.
- Swap 1 tablespoon of the olive oil for toasted sesame oil. Sprinkle with toasted sesame seeds before serving.
- Drizzle the warm roasted cabbage with hot honey.
- Brush the roasted cabbage with your favorite vinaigrette. Start with the balsamic vinaigrette on page 74.

Tips
- ✓ This recipe works best with a basic green or red cabbage. Softer cabbage varieties, such as Napa, Chinese, or savoy, are not ideal for roasting.
- ✓ Don't crowd the sheet pan. To get a lovely char, leave plenty of space on the pan. Without enough space, the cabbage will steam.

MAPLE MISO–GLAZED SWEET POTATOES

PREP: 15 minutes
COOK: 45 minutes
SERVES: 4

These miso-and-maple-roasted sweet potatoes are going to be your new favorite. These are not a swap for candied sweet potatoes, but I can confidently say that your family and friends will love it if you show up with these creamy, savory, and subtly sweet potatoes for Sunday dinner or the holidays. They also make a perfect side for a weeknight or special dinner.

Love Note

Miso is a thick paste of fermented soybeans, koji, and salt that is common in Japanese cuisine and provides both health benefits and a delicious umami flavor.

Ingredients

- 3 tablespoons coconut oil (unrefined) or butter (or vegan butter), melted
- 2 tablespoons maple syrup or brown sugar
- 2 tablespoons white miso
- 1 tablespoon apple cider vinegar
- ½ teaspoon chili sauce or hot sauce
- 1-inch piece fresh ginger, peeled and grated
- ¼ teaspoon coarse salt
- Black pepper, to taste
- 1 pound sweet potatoes, cut into about 2-inch pieces

Directions

1. Preheat the oven to 375°F.

2. In a medium bowl, whisk together all the ingredients except for the sweet potatoes, until well combined.

3. Add the cubed sweet potatoes to the bowl and toss to coat.

4. Spread the coated sweet potatoes into a single layer in an 8-by-8-inch baking dish.

5. Roast for 45 minutes, stirring once midway to distribute the glaze and avoid hot spots. When done, the sweet potatoes should be easily pierced with a fork and tender but not mushy.

Tips

✓ Peeling your potatoes is recommended but optional. Either way, be sure to scrub the potatoes under cool running water before cubing.
✓ You can find miso in tubs in the produce aisle of most major supermarkets and a wider variety at international supermarkets. It keeps for months in the refrigerator and can be used to add depth of flavor to a variety of plant-based dishes.

PAN-SEARED BEANS AND GREENS

PREP: 5 minutes
COOK: 15 minutes
SERVES: 4

This is the side that eats like a meal. The butter beans I ate growing up were simply stewed with ham hocks, onion, and seasonings—sometimes served with biscuits. This recipe is different. You might notice the Spanish influence here, as it was inspired by my trip to Barcelona. Now I cook some form of beans and greens regularly for a quick side dish, or pair them with rice for a full meal. This one smells *amazing*. The secret is in the first step of the recipe. Blooming the smoked paprika in the olive oil effectively infuses smoky flavor throughout the dish. Believe me, you'll make this one over and over again.

Ingredients

- 3 tablespoons extra-virgin olive oil, divided
- 2 garlic cloves, peeled and minced
- ½ teaspoon smoked paprika
- 1 (16-ounce) can large butter beans, drained and rinsed (or 2 cups cooked)
- 4 cups baby kale (about 4 ounces)
- 2 tablespoons vegetable broth or water
- ¼ to ½ teaspoon salt, to taste
- ¼ teaspoon freshly cracked black pepper
- Hot sauce for topping (optional but highly recommended)

Directions

1. In a large skillet, heat 2 tablespoons of the olive oil over medium heat. Add the garlic and smoked paprika. Stir for 1 to 2 minutes, until fragrant. Take care not to burn the garlic.

2. Add the butter beans in an even layer. Let cook undisturbed for about 2 minutes, until the beans start to sear. Then gently toss to coat with the oil and spice mixture. Transfer to a serving dish and set aside.

3. Heat the remaining 1 tablespoon of olive oil in the skillet over medium heat. Add the kale, broth or water, salt, and pepper. Cover and cook until the kale is just tender, about 5 to 7 minutes.

4. Gently combine the beans and greens. Serve warm.

Tips

✓ You can substitute mustard or turnip greens, or spinach, for the baby kale. Be sure to adjust the cook time: Reduce the cook time for spinach or soft greens; increase the time for heartier greens. Canned butter beans will be soft. Take care not to overcook them.

✓ Substitute chickpeas, cannellini beans, or other large white beans if you can't find butter beans.

Love Note

Just one tablespoon of sesame seeds provides 7 percent of the daily value for calcium plus other minerals, healthy fats, and protein.

SESAME-BLISTERED SHISHITOS

PREP: 5 minutes
COOK: 5 minutes
SERVES: 4

Though they can be hot, most shishito peppers are as mild as a green bell pepper. For this super-simple dish, I like using a hot cast-iron skillet to get a nice char on the peppers. This recipe has only a few ingredients, but the char might be the most important part of developing the flavor you'll savor.

Ingredients

- 2 cups small shishito peppers
- 1 tablespoon toasted sesame oil
- 1 to 2 tablespoons black or rice vinegar, to taste
- ¼ teaspoon coarse salt
- 2 tablespoons toasted sesame seeds

Directions

1. Rinse and dry the shishito peppers well with a clean kitchen towel. Don't skip this step: Drying the peppers helps to get a nice char and reduce hot oil splatters.

2. In a medium cast-iron skillet, heat the sesame oil over high heat until hot.

3. Working in batches to avoid crowding, add the peppers to the skillet. Cook 2 minutes on high, then flip the peppers or shake the skillet to turn. Cook for another 2 minutes or until the skins are blistered.

4. Toss the warm peppers with the vinegar and salt, then sprinkle with the toasted sesame seeds. Enjoy warm.

 Tips
- ✓ Enjoy as a side dish to fish, chicken, or tofu, or as an appetizer or snack.
- ✓ Shishitos are one of the easiest peppers to grow in an in-ground or container garden in the summer.

HONEY NUT– ROASTED BRUSSELS SPROUTS

PREP: **10 minutes**
COOK: **25 minutes**
SERVES: **4**

I'm a firm believer that roasting is the best way to cook brussels sprouts (though a shaved brussels sprout salad comes in a close second). The crispy, caramelized finish is packed with flavor that's only enhanced by this sweet and savory combination of honey, mustard, and a hint of soy sauce. You'll be tempted to eat these hot, straight from the sheet pan, but save some to serve alongside broiled salmon or as the star of an epic veggie plate.

Love Note

Brussels sprouts provide 12 percent of the daily recommendation of omega-3 fatty acids for women and 9 percent for men.

Ingredients

- 2 tablespoons spicy brown mustard
- 1 teaspoon whole-grain mustard
- 3 tablespoons honey
- 1 tablespoon soy sauce, tamari, or coconut aminos
- 4 cups baby brussels sprouts, trimmed and halved (about 1 pound)
- ¼ to ½ teaspoon salt
- ¼ teaspoon freshly ground black pepper
- ½ cup pecan halves

Directions

1. Preheat the oven to 400°F. Line a baking sheet with parchment paper or a silicone baking mat.

2. In a medium bowl, whisk together the brown mustard, whole-grain mustard, honey, and soy sauce.

3. Add the brussels sprouts, salt, and pepper to the bowl. Toss to coat.

4. Spread the brussels sprouts in a single layer onto a baking sheet. Don't crowd the pan. Roast for 20 to 25 minutes, or until the sprouts are lightly browned, turning once midway.

5. While the brussels sprouts roast, toast the pecans: Add the pecans to a dry skillet. Stir over medium-low heat until fragrant and lightly toasted, about 5 to 7 minutes.

6. Gently toss together the cooked brussels sprouts and toasted pecans. Serve warm.

Tips
- ✓ Mustard tends to be salty. Start with ¼ teaspoon of salt and add more if needed.
- ✓ Roasted brussels sprouts are best eaten fresh. They will keep about 2 days in the refrigerator. To reheat, spread in a single layer in the toaster oven for best results.

COMFORTING DRINKS AND DESSERTS

BLUEBERRY CREAM POPS

PREP: 5 minutes
COOK: 15 minutes + 4 to 6 hours to freeze
MAKES: 8 pops

Made with whole blueberries, coconut milk, and sugar to bring the flavors together, these fun freezer pops are a bright and refreshing addition to any summer day. The swirls remind me of one of the few candies I liked as a child—blueberry-and-vanilla-cream swirl pops. Using coconut milk adds a tropical flair and makes these pops dairy free while maintaining a creamy texture.

Love Note

Blueberries have one of the highest levels of antioxidants among commonly eaten fruits in the United States. The antioxidant polyphenol has been shown to decrease blood pressure, a major risk factor for cardiovascular disease.

Ingredients

- 2 cups fresh or frozen blueberries
- 1 tablespoon lemon juice
- 4 tablespoons sugar or more to taste, divided
- 1/8 teaspoon salt
- 1 (13.5-ounce) can full-fat coconut milk
- 1 teaspoon vanilla extract

Directions

1. In a small saucepan, cook the blueberries, lemon juice, 2 tablespoons of the sugar, and the salt over medium heat until the berries begin to pop and release their liquid, about 10 to 12 minutes. Let cool slightly. Puree, using an immersion blender or heat-safe blender, until smooth. The consistency should be of a not-so-thick smoothie.

2. For a uniform finish (recommended): Add the coconut milk, the remaining 2 tablespoons of sugar, and the vanilla extract to the blender. Blend until smooth.

3. Pour the mixture into ice-pop molds. Freeze for 4 to 6 hours or overnight.

4. To remove the frozen pops, dip the mold in hot water to loosen the pops. Gently tug on the sticks to pull each pop from the mold. Serve immediately.

VARIATIONS:

- For a swirled effect, in a separate small pot, heat the coconut milk over medium-low heat with the remaining 2 tablespoons of sugar, stirring consistently just until the sugar is fully dissolved. After pureeing the blueberry mix, fill the molds by alternating the blueberry and coconut mixtures. Freeze.

Tips

✓ Adjust the sugar to the sweetness of the berries and your personal preference.
✓ Swap the granulated sugar for coconut sugar, maple syrup, or honey if desired. Note that coconut sugar might take longer to dissolve into the blueberry mixture.

MY CHAI CONCENTRATE

PREP: 0 minutes
COOK: 25 minutes
MAKES: 4 cups

If you've spent any time with me online or in real life, you know I love tea and warm drinks. I started drinking chai 20 years ago after trying a popular boxed tea brand. I've learned a lot since then, including how to make my own concentrate to keep on hand for warm or cold drinks. With origins in present-day India, chai—a combination of black tea and warming spices—is now enjoyed around the world. My version is not based on one tradition but instead reflects my preferred blend. It offers an intense spice flavor with some heat from fresh ginger. The fragrance fills the house with a warm and comforting aroma that's a recipe for relaxation.

Ingredients

- 10 green cardamom pods, gently crushed
- 8 whole black peppercorns
- 8 whole cloves
- 4 cinnamon sticks
- 2 star anise pods
- 4 cups water
- 2-inch piece fresh ginger, sliced, not peeled
- 4 rooibos or black tea bags (or 3 tablespoons loose-leaf tea)
- 2 tablespoons maple syrup (or more to taste)
- ½ teaspoon vanilla extract
- Your favorite milk, for serving (see tips)

Directions

1. Toast the spices: Place the cardamom pods, peppercorns, cloves, cinnamon sticks, and star anise in a medium saucepan and heat over medium heat for 3 to 5 minutes until fragrant.

2. Add the water and ginger. Bring to a boil. Reduce the heat to medium-low, cover, and simmer for about 15 minutes. Remove from the heat. Add the tea bags and steep for 5 minutes.

3. Remove the tea bags and strain the liquid into a bowl or large heat-safe measuring cup. Stir in the maple syrup and vanilla extract. Let cool. Store in an airtight container in the refrigerator for up to a week.

4. To make a hot or cold chai latte, combine one part concentrate with one part milk.

Love Note

Rooibos tea is naturally caffeine free. A mug of rooibos tea is rich in antioxidants, thanks to the flavonoids aspalathin and nothofagin, which have anti-inflammatory properties.

Tips
- ✓ Remove the tea bags and steep the spices longer (up to 1 hour) to intensify the flavor.
- ✓ For a lovely latte, froth warm oat or whole milk in a cup. Pour an equal amount of warm concentrate into the cup. Sprinkle with a dash of ground cinnamon or cardamom.
- ✓ Freeze extra concentrate as ice cubes. Use these instead of regular ice in a cold chai drink so that your tea is never watered down.

SIMPLEST GREEN SMOOTHIE

PREP: 5 minutes
COOK: 0 minutes
MAKES: 2 smoothies

A trusty green smoothie recipe is essential for any plant-forward plan. It's an easy way to get a veggie boost first thing in the morning and the perfect way to use up overripe bananas. I like sprinkling in hemp seeds for staying power. Just three tablespoons of shelled hemp seeds deliver a full 10 grams of plant protein, plus healthy fats and fiber. Super satisfying—say goodbye to protein powder!

Ingredients

- 1½ cups plant milk
- 2 cups fresh baby spinach
- ½ cup frozen banana slices (1 small)
- ½ cup frozen pineapple
- 2 tablespoons hemp seeds or nut butter

Directions

Place all the ingredients in a top-down blender in the order listed. Blend until smooth.

VARIATIONS:

- Want a different fruit flavor? Swap in ½ to 1 cup of fresh mango or frozen berries for the pineapple.
- Can't do banana? Toss in a few pitted dates to sweeten your smoothie.
- Add some spice by blending in a small, peeled knob of fresh ginger.

Love Note

Bananas are a natural source of prebiotics, which help feed the healthy bacteria in the gut to potentially boost digestive health.

Tips
- ✓ Try soy, almond, cashew, or refrigerated coconut milk in this recipe. Oat and pea protein milk produce very frothy results.
- ✓ Use your brown bananas! Peel, slice, and freeze overripe bananas in a single layer on a tray, then transfer to a freezer-safe container. Now you have sweet, ripe bananas ready for smoothies, oats, and baked goods!

CREAMY CARDAMOM AND CASHEW COFFEE

PREP: 5 minutes
COOK: 5 minutes (plus overnight soak)
SERVES: 2

This just-sweet-enough, super-smooth coffee is creamy without any cream. The secret? A blender, soaked cashews, and black coffee. Whirl these with a dash of spice, maple syrup, and vanilla for a delightful coffee break. Best known for its ability to perk you up and boost athletic performance, coffee in optimal amounts may also help lower your risk for several chronic conditions.

Ingredients

- 2 cups quality brewed coffee
- ¼ cup raw cashews (soaked overnight and drained)
- 1 tablespoon maple syrup
- ½ teaspoon vanilla extract
- ¼ teaspoon ground cardamom or cinnamon

Directions

Put all the ingredients in a heat-safe high-speed blender. Blend until frothy. Pour and serve immediately.

Love Note

Cardamom is used in both sweet and savory dishes to provide a warm, fruity, and minty flavor. It is known as the "queen of spices" and is the third most expensive spice after vanilla and saffron.

Tip ✓ If you don't usually take sugar in your coffee, feel free to eliminate the maple syrup.

Love Note

The flavanols in dark chocolate have been shown to help improve blood pressure.

PEANUT BUTTER AND CHOCOLATE COOKIE SKILLET

PREP: 5 minutes
COOK: 25 minutes
SERVES: 8

Warm, gooey, peanut buttery, and a little chocolaty, this skillet is fun and easy to make. With oats as the base, it's healthy enough for breakfast yet sweet enough for dessert. Be sure to use overripe bananas for maximum sweetness and moisture. The best part: You can do all the mixing in a blender!

Ingredients

- 1 cup very overripe banana (2 medium bananas), mashed
- ½ cup plain oat or other plant milk
- ¼ cup brown sugar
- ¼ cup runny, natural peanut butter
- 1 teaspoon vanilla extract
- 2 cups traditional rolled oats
- 2 teaspoons ground cinnamon
- 2 teaspoons baking powder
- ½ teaspoon salt
- 2 ounces chocolate chunks

Directions

1. Preheat the oven to 350°F. Grease an 8-inch cast-iron skillet (or oven-safe pan) with butter or oil to prevent sticking. Set aside.

2. Using a small blender, puree the banana, plant milk, brown sugar, peanut butter, and vanilla extract until smooth and creamy.

3. Add the oats, cinnamon, baking powder, and salt. Blend for 20 to 30 seconds, until the oats are just incorporated and the mixture is smooth. Do not overmix.

4. Pour the batter into the prepared skillet. Top with the chocolate chunks.

5. Bake for 20 to 25 minutes, or until set. Be careful not to overcook it. Serve warm.

Tips
- ✓ If you prefer sweeter desserts, add another ¼ cup of brown sugar.
- ✓ Top with dark chocolate for a healthier twist.

CREAMY BANANA-NUT SMOOTHIE

PREP: 5 minutes
COOK: 0 minutes
MAKES: 2 smoothies

Are you putting walnuts in your smoothies? If not, you're missing out! With its rich and creamy texture, this smoothie reminds me of the banana-nut milkshakes I got as a kid from the only ice-cream shop in town. This smoothie delivers decadence in a different way— from the walnuts. It's naturally sweet and nutty with notes of caramel from the dates. The frozen banana whips into a frothy delight that you'll love sipping daily.

Ingredients

- 1 cup plain oat milk or other plant milk
- 2 small frozen overripe bananas, sliced
- ¼ cup toasted walnut pieces
- 1 Medjool date, pitted
- ½ teaspoon vanilla extract
- ¼ teaspoon ground cinnamon

Directions

1. Place all the ingredients in a blender in the order listed.
2. Blend until smooth and frothy.

Love Note

Dates sweeten smoothies without sugar. Just two Medjool dates provide over 3 grams of fiber, as well as plenty of potassium and magnesium.

Tips
✓ Add more or less milk to achieve the desired consistency.
✓ Save your overripe bananas for a smoothie day! Peel brown bananas, slice or break them in half, freeze in a single layer, store in a freezer-safe container, and use within 3 months.

CHERRY ALMOND CRISP

PREP: 15 minutes
COOK: 45 minutes + 20 minutes to rest
SERVES: 6 to 8

This is one of my favorite desserts. It's elegant enough to serve at a dinner party, yet packed with enough fruit and oats that you can enjoy leftovers for breakfast the next day. The buttery, crispy bits are balanced by a lightly sweetened bubbly and fragrant cherry filling. Add a dollop of ice cream or yogurt for a creamy finish. This easy recipe can be made with fresh or frozen cherries and can be doubled or cut in half—though you'll definitely want more.

Love Note

Dark, sweet cherries are packed with antioxidant and anti-inflammatory compounds that may help reduce the risk of certain chronic diseases.

Ingredients

CHERRY FILLING:
- 8 cups fresh or frozen cherries
- ¼ cup sugar
- 2 tablespoons arrowroot powder, all-purpose flour, tapioca flour, or cornstarch
- 2 teaspoons lemon zest, plus more for garnish
- 2 teaspoons vanilla extract

OAT-ALMOND TOPPING:
- 1 cup old-fashioned oats
- ½ cup slivered almonds, chopped
- ½ cup brown sugar or coconut sugar
- Pinch of salt
- ¼ cup cold unsalted regular butter (or vegan butter), cut into cubes
- Dollop of vanilla yogurt or ice cream (optional)

Directions

1. Heat the oven to 350°F. Place a 1-quart baking dish on a baking sheet lined with tinfoil.

2. **Make the cherry filling.** Put all the ingredients in the baking dish. Stir to combine.

3. **Make the oat-almond topping.** In a medium bowl, combine the oats, almonds, sugar, and salt. Using a pastry cutter, a fork, or your hands, cut the butter into the oat mixture until it takes on a crumb-like appearance.

4. Mound the crisp topping over the cherry filling. Bake until the juices bubble and the topping is golden brown, 35 to 45 minutes. Let it rest for at least 20 minutes to set. Sprinkle with optional lemon zest. Serve warm with the yogurt or ice cream, if desired.

Tips
- ✓ This recipe reheats well in the oven.
- ✓ No almonds? Swap in pecans in the same amount.
- ✓ Be sure to choose blanched or slivered almonds–whole almonds (with the skin) will not incorporate well.

WARM COCONUT RICE PUDDING

PREP: 5 minutes
COOK: 30 minutes
SERVES: 8

Subtly sweet and perfectly spiced, this warm rice pudding is a comforting dessert that you'll want to cozy up to time and again. The coconut milk makes this rice pudding so creamy and adds a fruity twist. This easy dessert is 100 percent plant-based, making it an ideal recipe to serve to guests. Top with fresh mango or other fruit for an elegant presentation, and your guests will think you've been in the kitchen all day!

Ingredients

- 1 cup uncooked long-grain white rice
- 2 (13.5-ounce) cans full-fat coconut milk
- 1 cup water
- ⅓ cup sugar
- ¼ teaspoon salt
- 5 cardamom pods, cracked
- 1 cinnamon stick
- 1 teaspoon vanilla extract (optional)
- Mango or other fruit, for garnish
- Cinnamon sticks or ground cinnamon, for garnish

Directions

1. Toast the rice in a large, dry 3-quart saucepan over medium-high heat. Gently shake the pan or stir the rice occasionally until fragrant and lightly golden, about 5 to 7 minutes. Add the coconut milk, water, sugar, salt, cardamom, and cinnamon stick. Stir to combine.

2. Bring the mixture to a low boil, stirring frequently to make sure the rice doesn't clump.

3. Reduce the heat to low. Simmer uncovered for 20 to 25 minutes, stirring occasionally, until the rice is tender and most of the liquid has been absorbed, leaving a creamy consistency.

4. Remove the pan from the heat. Remove the cardamom pods and cinnamon stick. If using the vanilla extract, stir it in now.

5. Serve warm, topped with the mango and cinnamon.

Tips
- ✓ Don't have whole spices? Substitute 1 teaspoon ground cardamom plus a pinch of nutmeg, ginger, or cinnamon for the cardamom pods and cinnamon sticks.
- ✓ The rice pudding will thicken as it cools. It can be enjoyed cold. To reheat, add a splash of milk, cover, and microwave on medium power, about 1 to 1½ minutes, until the pudding is easily stirred and warm, not hot.
- ✓ Got leftovers? Refrigerate any leftover pudding for up to 5 days in an airtight container.

BROWN BUTTER PISTACHIO COOKIES

PREP: 10 minutes + 1 hour 30 minutes to chill
COOK: 18 to 20 minutes
MAKES: 1 dozen cookies

I tend to like cookies that have a good balance of sweet and savory. Because these cookies are covered in powdered sugar, they get plenty of sweetness without adding too much sugar to the cookie dough. That sweet-but-not-too-sweet flavor is balanced by salty pistachios and rich brown butter.

Love Note

Skip the plastic wrap and cover your bowl of dough with a tight-fitting plate or reusable beeswax wrap, or place the dough in a reusable bag.

Tips

✓ Prefer a gluten-free cookie? Swap in a gluten-free baking flour 1:1 for the all-purpose flour. Pop the rolled cookies in the freezer for 10 minutes before baking.

✓ For 100 percent plant-based cookies, use vegan butter and vegan powdered sugar. Many vegan butters won't brown, so skip step 1; soften the butter and go straight to step 2.

Ingredients

- ½ cup unsalted butter (1 stick)
- ¾ cup powdered sugar, divided
- 1 teaspoon vanilla extract
- ¼ teaspoon coarse salt
- 1 cup all-purpose flour
- ½ cup crushed and toasted pistachios

Directions

1. To make the brown butter, melt the butter in a thick-bottomed skillet over medium heat, whisking frequently. After the butter starts to foam, watch for small browned bits to form and a nutty aroma. Remove from the heat and immediately transfer the brown butter to a medium mixing bowl. Refrigerate for 30 minutes—until the butter starts to resolidify but is still soft enough to whip.

2. Using a hand mixer on medium speed, cream the soft brown butter and ¼ cup powdered sugar until light and fluffy.

3. Beat in the vanilla extract until evenly incorporated. Scrape down the sides of the bowl as needed.

4. Beat in the salt and most of the flour on low speed, until the dough forms.

5. Fold in the pistachios until the dough is smooth and the nuts are evenly incorporated. Cover tightly and refrigerate dough for at least 1 hour, or until dough is firm.

6. Once the dough is firm, preheat the oven to 350°F. Line a baking sheet with parchment paper or a silicone baking mat.

7. Using a tablespoon or small scoop, form 12 1-inch dough balls. Place each about 1 inch apart on the baking sheet. Bake for 18 to 20 minutes, or until the cookies are lightly golden. Let cool for about 5 minutes on the baking sheet.

8. Place the remaining ½ cup powdered sugar in a medium bowl. Gently toss the warm cookies in the sugar until dusted all over. Place on a wire rack to cool completely.

9. Store leftovers in a sealed container at room temperature for up to 5 days or freeze for up to 3 months. To serve from frozen, thaw cookies on a wire rack at room temperature and dust with extra powdered sugar.

MANGO SOFT SERVE

PREP: 15 minutes
COOK: 0 minutes
MAKES: 6 cups

This rich and creamy dessert will transport your taste buds to the tropics. Sweet and juicy mango is the perfect base for a refreshing sorbet whipped up easily at home. Made of mostly mango, this is a tasty way to get a hefty dose of vitamin C. Serve it after a spicy meal or as a way to cool down at a cookout.

Ingredients

- 3 cups frozen mango cut into ½-inch cubes
- ¾ cup full-fat coconut milk, at room temperature, shaken
- 3 tablespoons honey (or agave nectar if vegan)
- 2 teaspoons fresh lime juice
- ⅛ teaspoon coarse salt
- Toasted coconut chips or flakes, for garnish

Directions

1. In a food processor, combine the frozen mango, coconut milk, honey, lime juice, and salt. Pulse until the mango is chopped small.

2. Process, scraping down the sides as needed, until it's smooth and has a whipped texture, about 3 minutes.

3. Serve immediately. For presentation, press the mango puree into a large plastic bag. Trim off one corner and pipe into serving bowls. Garnish with toasted coconut chips or flakes.

Love Note

Mango provides lutein and zeaxanthin, two carotenoids that may help support eye health.

Tips

✓ Use full-fat coconut milk, which typically comes in a can–not the refrigerated kind.
✓ Don't have a food processor? Use a high-powered blender.
✓ Peel, slice, and freeze your own mango or make it easy on yourself: Buy precut, frozen mango chunks.

COCOA ALMOND TRUFFLES

PREP: 15 minutes + 30 minutes in freezer
COOK: 0 minutes
MAKES: 16 truffles

These cocoa-almond truffles are super simple to make and definitely worth pulling out the food processor for. With a rich chocolate flavor, these nourishing bites also have some nutritional benefits: The almonds deliver satisfying plant protein and good fat, cocoa powder is packed with flavonoids that may help heart and brain health, and dates bind the truffles with a natural sweetness. This recipe can be made with pantry staples, and I love keeping a batch on hand for an energizing snack or a healthy dessert.

Love Note

Cocoa is an abundant source of flavanols that may play a role in improving mood and cognitive function.

Ingredients

- 10 plump pitted Medjool dates, at room temperature
- 1 cup whole roasted, unsalted almonds
- ¼ cup unsweetened cocoa powder, divided
- 1 teaspoon espresso powder (optional)
- ½ teaspoon vanilla extract
- Pinch of sea salt
- 2 tablespoons water (if needed)

Directions

1. Line a sheet pan with parchment paper.

2. Put the dates, almonds, 2 tablespoons of the cocoa powder, the espresso powder (if using), vanilla extract, and salt in a food processor. Pulse until the dates and almonds are chopped. Run the food processor on high until all ingredients are incorporated and a sticky ball forms. If the mixture doesn't come together after a minute, slowly add up to 2 tablespoons of water, a little bit at a time, until it forms a sticky ball.

3. Using wet hands, portion out a heaping tablespoon of the almond-date mixture and roll it into a ball. Repeat until you have about 16 balls.

4. Place them on the sheet pan. Freeze to set, about 30 minutes.

5. Add the remaining 2 tablespoons of cocoa powder to a small bowl. To finish, toss or roll each ball in the bowl until fully dusted with cocoa powder. Serve.

6. Refrigerate any leftovers in a sealed container for up to a week, or freeze for longer storage (up to 3 months). Let the frozen truffles stand at room temperature to thaw before eating (about 15 minutes).

Tips
✓ Make sure your dates are fresh. If they are starting to dry out, you'll likely need to add water to help the mixture stick.
✓ Be sure to choose unsweetened cocoa powder for this recipe, not a cocoa powder mix that might include other ingredients.
✓ Don't have espresso powder? Leave it out. Espresso powder enhances the chocolate flavor but isn't required.

Produce by Season

While it's possible to get almost any food at any time, eating by seasons has its perks. It can inspire creativity. Also, local fresh produce can be less expensive and may retain more of some nutrients thanks to shorter travel distance from field to fork.

I compiled this guide as a resource to inspire you to explore new foods. But whether they are farm fresh or from the frozen food aisle, my hope is for you to put plenty of plants on your plate with ease.

Depending on where you are in the world, your growing season may differ from this guide. Check with your local extension service, grocery store produce manager, or local farmers to discover when your favorite produce will peak.

Spring

Apricots	Collard greens	Lemons	Sweet peas
Artichokes	Dandelion greens	Lettuce	Pineapples
Arugula	Garlic	Limes	Radishes
Asparagus	Fava beans	Mangoes	Ramps
Avocados	Fennel	Mushrooms	Rhubarb
Bananas	Fiddleheads	Mustard greens	Serviceberries (juneberries)
Beets	Herbs	New potatoes	Spinach
Bok choy	Kale	Vidalia onions	Strawberries
Broccoli	Kohlrabi	Parsnips	Swiss chard
Cabbage	Kiwifruit	Snap and snow peas	Turnips
Carrots	Leeks	Spinach	
Celery			

Fall

Apples	Collard greens	Limes	Quince
Avocados	Figs	Mushrooms	Rutabagas
Bananas	Grapefruit	Onions	Shallots
Beets	Herbs (rosemary, oregano, sage)	Oranges	Sweet potatoes and yams
Brussels sprouts	Horseradish	Parsnips	Swiss chard
Butternut squash	Kale	Pears	Turnips and turnip greens
Cabbage	Kiwifruit	Persimmons	Winter squash
Carrots	Leeks	Pineapples	
Celery	Lemons	Potatoes	
Chicory		Pumpkin	

Summer

Apples	Chard	Herbs (basil, cilantro, parsley, lovage)	Raspberries
Apricots	Cherries		Shelling beans
Avocados	Chayote squash	Honeydew	Shishito peppers
Bananas	Chilies	Jackfruit	Strawberries
Beets	Cucumbers	Lemons	Summer squash
Bell peppers	Currants	Lima beans	Sunchokes
Blackberries	Eggplant	Limes	Sweet corn
Blueberries	Fennel	Mangoes	Tomatillos
Boysenberries	Figs	Nectarines	Tomatoes
Breadfruit	Garlic	Okra	Watermelon
Cantaloupe	Grapes	Peaches	
Carrots	Green beans	Plums and pluots	
Celery	Green onions		

Winter

Apples	Collard greens	Limes	Rutabagas
Avocados	Cranberries	Meyer lemons	Sweet potatoes and yams
Bananas	Grapefruit	Onions	Tangerines
Blood oranges	Herbs (rosemary, thyme)	Oranges	Turnips
Brussels sprouts	Kale	Parsnips	Winter squash
Cabbage	Kiwifruit	Pears	
Cara cara oranges	Kumquats	Pineapples	
Carrots	Leeks	Pomegranates	
Celery	Lemons	Potatoes	

Year-round

Because they are grown in tropical regions,
many foods such as bananas, passion fruit, and papayas
are available all year long.

NUTRITIONAL INFORMATION

Serving sizes listed below are a point of reference or to consider carbohydrate intake. They do not define how much you should eat.

Recipe	Page	Serving Size	Calories	Total Fat (in grams)	Saturated Fat (in grams)	Trans Fat (in grams)	Cholesterol (in milligrams)	Total Carbohydrates (in grams)	Dietary Fiber (in grams)	Total Sugars (in grams)	Protein (in grams)
Pecan Butter	66	2 tbsp	89	9	1	0	0	3	1	2	1
Strawberry Chia Jam	67	1 tbsp	11	0	0	0	0	2	1	1	0
Oat Milk	69	¾ cup	88	1	0	0	0	17	3	3	3
Nut Milk	69	1 cup	81	5	0.5	0	0	9	1	7	2
Hemp Milk	69	1 cup	90	6	0.5	0	0	4	6	3	5
Peanut Sauce	70	2 tbsp	122	8	1.5	0	0	7	1	5	4
Lime Ranch Dressing	70	2 tbsp	14	1	0.5	0	2	1	0	1	1
Blender Salsa	71	2 tbsp	14	0	0	0	0	3	1	1	1
Chipotle Mayo	71	1 tbsp	48	5	1	0	3	0	0	0	0
Kale Walnut Pesto	72	2 tbsp	168	18	3.5	0	3	1	1	0	3
Vegan Pesto	72	2 tbsp	301	32	5	0	0	4	2	0	3
Basic Balsamic Vinaigrette	74	2 tbsp	190	21	3.5	0	0	3	0	3	0
Lemon Vinaigrette	74	2 tbsp	162	19	3	0	0	1	0	0	0
Taco Seasoning	75	¼ tsp	2	0	0	0	0	0	0	0	0
BBQ Seasoning	75	¼ tsp	4	0	0	0	0	1	0	0	0
Baked Eggs and Greens	81	1 egg + about 1 cup vegetables	282	23	6	0	199	11	2	7	11
Make-Ahead Spinach Breakfast Wraps	83	1 wrap	379	18	6.5	0	189	39	3	4	14
Chickpea Breakfast Scramble	84	½ cup	183	8	1	0	0	22	5	1	5
Savory Quinoa Breakfast Bowls	85	1 bowl	507	34	5.5	0	175	41	11	5	16
Walnut Breakfast Patties	86	1 patty	197	17	2	0	22	9	2	2	5
Nutty Caramelized Banana and Steel-Cut Oats	87	¾ cup oats + ½ banana + ½ tbsp peanut butter	396	19	7	0	23	46	6	8	10

NUTRITIONAL INFORMATION

Recipe	Page	Serving Size	Calories	Total Fat (in grams)	Saturated Fat (in grams)	Trans Fat (in grams)	Cholesterol (in milligrams)	Total Carbohydrates (in grams)	Dietary Fiber (in grams)	Total Sugars (in grams)	Protein (in grams)
Caramelized Pears With Walnuts and Yogurt	90	2 pear halves + ¼ cup yogurt + 2 tbsp walnuts	311	12	2	0	8	44	7	31	8
Peach Almond Baked Oatmeal	91	½ cup	201	6	2	0	26	30	4	10	7
Blueberry Buttermilk Oat Muffins	93	1 muffin	168	5	3	0	26	27	2	12	4
Fully Loaded Breakfast Cookies	95	1 cookie	210	13	1.5	0	1	20	4	10	5
Fruit and Oat Bars	99	1 bar	324	13	5.5	0	0	46	7	21	6
BBQ-Roasted Black-Eyed Peas	101	¼ cup	167	8	1	0	0	19	3	3	7
Rosemary-Roasted Walnuts	103	¼ cup	195	20	2	0	0	4	2	1	4
Parmesan Zucchini Crisps	105	about 1½ cups	223	18	4	0	10	8	3	4	11
Peanut Chili Crunch Popcorn	107	about 2 cups	307	27	3.5	0	0	16	4	1	4
No-Bake Almond Berry Bars	109	1 bar	157	11	1	0	0	12	4	7	5
Sweet and Salty Pepita Granola	111	¼ cup	188	13	2	0	0	12	3	6	8
Fresh Peach Caprese	115	about 1 cup	251	20	6.5	0	20	15	2	8	7
Brown Rice and Cabbage Crunch Salad	117	1¾ cups	432	29	5	0	0	35	6	9	13
Strawberry, Arugula, and Pistachio Salad	119	½ of the salad	690	53	12.5	0	33	42	9	26	17
Mushroom Ricotta Toast	121	1 toast	250	11	3	0	10	30	4	4	11
Chickpea and Rice Soup	122	about 2½ cups	423	10	1	0	0	72	11	9	11
Warm Roasted Broccoli Salad	123	1¼ cups	256	21	3	0	0	17	3	12	4

NUTRITIONAL INFORMATION

Recipe	Page	Serving Size	Calories	Total Fat (in grams)	Saturated Fat (in grams)	Trans Fat (in grams)	Cholesterol (in milligrams)	Total Carbohydrates (in grams)	Dietary Fiber (in grams)	Total Sugars (in grams)	Protein (in grams)
Herbed Cauliflower and White Bean Soup	126	1½ cups + 1 tsp oil + 1 tbsp walnuts + ¼ cup croutons	461	27	4	0	0	44	11	7	13
Smashed Chickpea Salad Sandwich	127	1 sandwich	295	10	1.5	0	0	41	7	6	9
Pesto White Bean Veggie Wrap	128	1 wrap	508	25	5	0	0	60	9	4	14
Autumn Harvest Salad	129	about 1½ cups	415	21	2.5	0	0	54	10	13	8
Pesto Chickpea Bowls	131	1 bowl	320	18	3.5	0	177	28	5	2	14
Black Bean and Cheddar Burgers	133	1 burger	662	34	9.5	0	33	71	20	6	25
Watermelon Salad With Honey-Lime Vinaigrette	135	¾ cup	112	6	2	0	10	13	1	10	4
Black Bean and Spinach Quesadillas	137	1 quesadilla	362	12	5	0	14	48	9	2	16
Mushroom Cheesesteak	139	1 sandwich	397	22	9.5	0	35	38	3	10	15
Roasted Carrot Soup	141	1¼ cups	209	14	2.5	0	0	20	5	10	2
Peanut Stew	145	1½ cups + rice	370	17	3.5	0	0	47	8	10	10
Shrimp Succotash	147	about 1½ cups	235	8	2.5	0	79	31	5	6	14
Blended Chicken and Mushroom Meatballs	148	3 meatballs	266	13	3	0	129	13	2	2	25
Creamy Roasted Red Pepper Pasta	149	1 cup pasta + ½ cup sauce	556	32	4.5	0	0	60	9	10	14
Spinach Artichoke Flatbreads	151	1 flatbread	577	36	9	0	28	54	5	5	18

NUTRITIONAL INFORMATION

Recipe	Page	Serving Size	Calories	Total Fat (in grams)	Saturated Fat (in grams)	Trans Fat (in grams)	Cholesterol (in milligrams)	Total Carbohydrates (in grams)	Dietary Fiber (in grams)	Total Sugars (in grams)	Protein (in grams)
Mushroom and Lentil Bolognese	154	1 cup sauce + 1 cup cooked pasta + 1 tbsp cheese	397	10	2	0	4	66	10	9	15
Black Beans and Cheese Grits	155	1 cup grits + ¾ cup black beans	479	16	7	0	29	68	13	4	17
Cauliflower and Avocado Tacos	157	2 tacos	246	16	2	0	0	25	7	3	5
Tomato, Olive, and Arugula Frittata	159	¼ of the frittata	242	18	4	0	272	9	1	3	12
Rosemary-Roasted Salmon and Grapes	161	1 salmon fillet + ½ cup grapes + 1 cup greens	320	15	2.5	0	72	16	1	13	27
Quick Coconut Chickpea Stew	164	1½ cups	457	25	20.5	0	0	44	12	15	13
Winter Squash Red Curry	165	about 1 cup	498	24	15	0	0	53	13	10	18
Pinto Bean Cakes With Avocado Salsa	167	2 pinto cakes + ¼ of the salsa	490	22	3	0	0	61	21	5	16
One-Skillet Spinach and Mushroom Lasagna	169	1½ to 2 cups	399	18	6.5	0	27	43	6	9	17
Spinach and Ricotta Linguine	171	about 2 cups	587	16	3.5	0	8	94	7	5	20
Black Bean-Stuffed Sweet Plantains	172	½ stuffed plantain	431	10	2.5	0	5	78	15	28	13
Red Rice	173	about ¾ cup	432	17	5	0	28	56	4	8	12
Spicy BBQ Tofu Lettuce Cups	175	about 2 cups + lettuce leaves	232	11	1.5	0	0	24	4	15	11
Sheet Pan Fajitas	178	2 tortillas + fish mixture	341	12	3	0	43	35	4	6	23

NUTRITIONAL INFORMATION

Recipe	Page	Serving Size	Calories	Total Fat (in grams)	Saturated Fat (in grams)	Trans Fat (in grams)	Cholesterol (in milligrams)	Total Carbohydrates (in grams)	Dietary Fiber (in grams)	Total Sugars (in grams)	Protein (in grams)
Kale Slaw With Peanut Dressing	179	1 cup	260	21	2.5	0	0	15	4	1	7
Socca With Sautéed Vegetables	181	¼ of the socca and sautéed vegetables	227	10	1.5	0	0	29	7	3	9
Roasted Shrimp, Pineapple, and Pepper Tacos	183	2 tacos	366	12	2	0	147	45	6	14	23
Lentil-Stuffed Peppers	185	2 stuffed pepper halves	402	12	4	0	17	58	12	12	16
Crispy Okra	189	½ cup	69	4	0.5	0	0	9	4	2	2
Honey Pepper Broccoli	190	¾ cup	262	20	5.5	0	15	24	3	19	3
Chard With Tahini	191	½ cup	136	11	2	0	0	8	2	3	4
Nutty Roasted Cauliflower and Grapes	193	1 cup	230	14	2	0	2	22	5	13	7
Coconut-Braised Collard Greens	195	½ cup	98	8	4.5	0	0	5	2	1	2
Lemon-Walnut Roasted Asparagus	196	3 to 4 ounces	168	16	2.5	0	0	7	3	2	4
Simple Roasted Cabbage	197	1 wedge	112	7	1	0	0	10	4	6	2
Maple Miso–Glazed Sweet Potatoes	199	½ cup	238	11	9	0	0	34	4	13	3
Pan-Seared Beans and Greens	201	½ cup	201	12	2	0	0	21	8	1	6
Sesame-Blistered Shishitos	204	¾ cup	68	5	1	0	0	5	3	2	1
Honey Nut–Roasted Brussels Sprouts	205	¾ cup	182	9	1	0	0	23	5	15	4
Blueberry Cream Pops	209	1 pop	124	7	6.5	0	0	13	1	11	1

NUTRITIONAL INFORMATION

Recipe	Page	Serving Size	Calories	Total Fat (in grams)	Saturated Fat (in grams)	Trans Fat (in grams)	Choles-terol (in milli-grams)	Total Carbohy-drates (in grams)	Dietary Fiber (in grams)	Total Sugars (in grams)	Protein (in grams)
My Chai Concentrate	211	½ cup concentrate	14	0	0	0	0	3	0	3	0
Simplest Green Smoothie	213	about 1½ cups	225	8	1	0	0	33	6	13	8
Creamy Cardamom and Cashew Coffee	215	1 cup	112	6	1	0	0	11	1	7	3
Peanut Butter and Chocolate Cookie Skillet	218	1 wedge	250	9	3	0	0	38	5	13	6
Creamy Banana-Nut Smoothie	219	about 1 cup	276	12	1.5	0	0	41	5	23	5
Cherry Almond Crisp	221	about 1 cup	406	15	5.5	0	20	70	7	44	6
Warm Coconut Rice Pudding	223	½ cup	258	14	13	0	0	27	0	9	3
Brown Butter Pistachio Cookies	225	2 cookies	339	20	10	1	41	37	2	18	4
Mango Soft Serve	227	½ cup	58	2	2	0	0	10	0	8	0
Cocoa Almond Truffles	229	2 truffles	178	9	0.5	0	0	24	5	16	5

ACKNOWLEDGMENTS

I became a registered dietitian nutritionist because it marries three things I love: food, science, and helping people. And I know it's a privilege to call something I am so passionate about work.

Becoming an author has been on my professional bucket list for some time. I am grateful to everyone on the National Geographic team for helping to make my first cookbook a reality. A very special thanks first and foremost to Allyson Johnson for reaching out. Thanks for embracing and celebrating my plant-forward, eat-what-makes-you-feel-good approach and guiding me through the process of becoming an author. Thanks for the spot-on edits and insight throughout the writing process.

Thanks, Adrian Coakley, for your expert photography guidance and travel adventure stories to inspire my next trip. Thanks, Sanaa Akkach, for your creative direction. I treasure your style, warmth, expert artistic vision, and seemingly infinite supply of vintage props. Elisa Gibson, thanks for your vision, support, and enthusiasm throughout the process.

Thanks to the recipe-testing team, chef Rich Hannan and Lisa Gerry. It was a pleasure working together. Rich, thank you for testing each recipe and providing prompt, honest, and thorough feedback. And thanks to Andrea Kirkland for the swift and thorough nutritional analysis for each and every recipe in this book.

I appreciate everyone on the food- and prop-styling teams for your creativity and unbelievable organization and energy on those long shoot days. Thanks to Katelyn Hardwick, Lulu Gyoury, and Morgan Locke for your hard work.

Thanks to the talented photographer Scott Suchman and the team for making the cover shoot so much fun. Thanks to Pascale Lemaire for your wardrobe-styling expertise, energy, and insight and for gracing our shoot with your incredible Haitian rum cake. Thank you, Shauné Hayes, for flawless makeup and your expert iPhone videography, and Katoya Shaw for your fun and positive spirit.

I am grateful to my family and friends for endless support, love, and encouragement. Thank you for listening to me, being my informal taste testers, and being a mirror to keep recipes simple, approachable, and accessible. Thanks to my mom for gentle encouragement, Aunt Jackie for accountability, and my dad for being curious. Thanks to my grandmother, grandfather, and Aunt Debbie for showing me how to cook simple, fuss-free, tasty recipes using what's available—and for understanding how to eat with the seasons, preserve for later, and appreciate what each food has to offer.

Thanks to close friends who are like family for supporting me—even before this book became an option. Thanks for enduring countless days of recipe development, kitchen takeovers, and last-minute supermarket runs and for navigating a refrigerator packed with different versions of multiple recipes at any given time. A special thanks to K. Kelley for trying out recipes, long phone calls, and being my target audience taste tester. To every friend who has ever said a kind word, asked how the book is coming along, and rooted me on, I appreciate your encouragement and support.

I am grateful to my grandma and public access TV for teaching me how to cook before I ever knew that a career as a dietitian in food or media was a thing. Thank you for nurturing my love for good food. Thanks to Dr. Mildred "Missy" Cody for being the best food science professor—requiring recipe development with an eye for creating nutritious recipes that are also affordable as part of my undergraduate studies. Thanks to my adviser in the Office of Minority Educational Development at Georgia Tech for introducing me to the idea of becoming a dietitian before I knew the profession existed and while I was on a path to becoming a chemical engineer. Thanks for connecting the dots between me making smoothies in my dorm and the organic chemistry, physics, and calculus classes I enjoyed. I am forever grateful to Kathea Ash-Green for being the first Black dietitian I'd ever met, for letting me shadow you while I was just thinking about becoming an RD, and for years later continuing to encourage me to keep going.

Thanks to Chris Rosenbloom for encouraging me to pursue a nontraditional career in communications while I was still working full time at the Centers for Disease Control and Prevention. Doris Acosta and the team for selecting me for the Academy Spokesperson program and opening the door to a career in nutrition communications. Liz Spitler for assigning my first magazine writing gig and putting me in front of a camera with a script. Ed Jones for the flexibility to serve as an expert on CNN and pursue my graduate studies while working full time. And to the many colleagues and friends from CDC for an evidence-based, learning-focused work environment where I made friends for life who still celebrate and support my work. It's these experiences and teachings that helped lay the foundation for this book.

I'd like to extend a special thanks to colleague Emily Walker for your research assistance. And to Sharon B. for your support, candor, and invaluable insight.

To my growing community—those who I know in real life, those I feel like I know in real life, and those yet to connect—thanks for following along, signing up for my email list, making recipes, asking questions, sharing my content, and simply showing up! Thank you for sticking around when I retreated to work on this book and for checking on me when my social media breaks go a bit long.

To my readers, I believe this book will be a resource to help you discover your personal plant love story. It can help you discover your version of success, explore a new mindset around what you eat, put more plants on the plate, and try a few new ideas.

I am grateful for your support in shaping my work and the opportunity to serve.

SOURCES

Bui, Thi Nhumg, Thi Hop Le, Do Huy Nguyen, Quang Binh Tran, Thi Lam Nguyen, Danh Tuyen Le, Do Van Anh Nguyen, Anh Linh Vu, Hiromichi Aoto, Yasuhide Okuhara, Yukihiko Ito, Shigeru Yamamoto, and Mitsuo Kise. "Pre-Germinated Brown Rice Reduced Both Blood Glucose Concentration and Body Weight in Vietnamese Women With Impaired Glucose Tolerance." *Journal of Nutritional Science and Vitaminology* (2014), pubmed.ncbi.nlm.nih.gov/25078374.

Chaddha, Ashish, and Kim A. Eagle. "Omega-3 Fatty Acids and Heart Health." *Circulation* (December 1, 2015), www.ahajournals.org/doi/full/10.1161/CIRCULATIONAHA.114.015176.

Chung, T.Y., E.N. Nwokolo, and J.S. Sim. "Compositional and Digestibility Changes in Sprouted Barley and Canola Seeds." *Plant Foods for Human Nutrition* (September 1989), pubmed.ncbi.nlm.nih.gov/2608636.

Culinary Institute of America and Harvard T.H. Chan School of Public Health. Menus of Change. www.menusofchange.org.

Ghumman, Atinder, Amritpal Kaur, and Narpinder Singh. "Impact of Germination on Flour, Protein and Starch Characteristics of Lentil *(Lens culinari)* and Horsegram *(Macrotyloma uniflorum L.)* Lines." *LWT—Food Science and Technology* (August 6, 2015), sciencedirect.com/science/article/abs/pii/S002364381530092X.

Hefni, Mohammed, and Cornelia M. Witthöft. "Enhancement of the Folate Content in Egyptian Pita Bread." *Food and Nutrition Research* (April 2, 2012), pubmed.ncbi.nlm.nih.gov/22489220.

Hemler, Elena C., and Frank B. Hu. "Plant-Based Diets for Personal, Population, and Planetary Health." *Advances in Nutrition* (November 1, 2019), ncbi.nlm.nih.gov/pmc/articles/PMC6855934.

Hrynowski, Zach. "What Percentage of Americans Are Vegetarian?," Gallup.com, November 20, 2021, news.gallup.com/poll/267074/percentage-americans-vegetarian.aspx.

Hsu, Tzu-Fang, Mitsuo Kise, Ming-Fu Wang, Yukihiko Ito, Mie-Due Yang, Hiromichi Aoto, Rie Yoshihara , Jyunichi Yokoyama, Daisuke Kunii, and Shigeru Yamamoto. "Effects of Pre-Germinated Brown Rice on Blood Glucose and Lipid Levels in Free-Living Patients With Impaired Fasting Glucose or Type 2 Diabetes." *Journal of Nutritional Science and Vitaminology* (2008), pubmed.ncbi.nlm.nih.gov/18490847.

Huang, Jiaqi. "Association Between Plant and Animal Protein Intake and Overall and Cause-Specific Mortality." *JAMA Internal Medicine* (September 1, 2020), jamanetwork.com/journals/jamainternalmedicine/fullarticle/2768358.

Kim, Hyunju, Laura E. Caulfield, Vanessa Garcia-Larsen, Lyn M. Steffen, Josef Coresh, and Casey M. Rebholz. "Plant-Based Diets Are Associated With a Lower Risk of Incident Cardiovascular Disease, Cardiovascular Disease Mortality, and All-Cause Mortality in a General Population of Middle-Aged Adults." *Journal of the American Heart Association* (August 7, 2019), ahajournals.org/doi/10.1161/JAHA.119.012865.

Madigan, Mariah, and Elisa Karhu. "The Role of Plant-Based Nutrition in Cancer Prevention." *Journal of Unexplored Medical Data* (November 8, 2018), jumdjournal.net/article/view/2892.

Marrone, Giulia, Cristina Guerriero, Daniela Palazzetti, Paolo Lido, Alessandro Marolla, Francesca Di Daniele, and Annalisa Noce. "Vegan Diet Health Benefits in Metabolic Syndrome." *Nutrients* (March 2, 2021), ncbi.nlm.nih.gov/pmc/articles/PMC7999488.

McCarthy, Justin, and Scott DeKoster. "Nearly One in Four in U.S. Have Cut Back on Eating Meat." Gallup.com, November 20, 2021, news.gallup.com/poll/282779/nearly-one-four-cut-back-eating-meat.aspx.

Menus of Change. *Plant-Forward by the Numbers*. Culinary Institute of America and President and Fellows of Harvard College, www.ciaprochef.com/MOC/PFbytheNumbers.pdf/.

National Institutes of Health. "Calcium: Fact Sheet for Health Professionals." U.S. Department of Health and Human Services, updated November 17, 2021, ods.od.nih.gov/factsheets/Calcium-HealthProfessional.

———. "Iron: Fact Sheet for Health Professionals." U.S. Department of Health and Human Services, updated April 5, 2022, ods.od.nih.gov/factsheets/Iron-HealthProfessional.

———. "Vitamin B$_{12}$: Fact Sheet for Health Professionals." U.S. Department of Health and Human Services, updated March 9, 2022, ods.od.nih.gov/factsheets/VitaminB12-HealthProfessional.

———. "Zinc: Fact Sheet for Health Professionals." U.S. Department of Health and Human Services, updated December 7, 2021, ods.od.nih.gov/factsheets/Zinc-HealthProfessional/#en2.

Ou, Keqin, Yongqiang Cheng, Ying Xing, Li Lin, Robert Nout, and Jianfen Liang. "Phytase Activity in Brown Rice During Steeping and Sprouting." *Journal of Food Science and Technology* (October 2011), pubmed.ncbi.nlm.nih.gov/23572793.

Sarita and Ekta Singh. "Potential of Millets: Nutrient Composition and Health Benefits." *Journal of Scientific Innovation and Research* (2016), jsirjournal.com/Vol5_Issue2_04.pdf.

Shapira, Niva. "The Potential Contribution of Dietary Factors to Breast Cancer Prevention." *European Journal of Cancer Prevention* (September 2017), pubmed.ncbi.nlm.nih.gov/28746163.

Tomova, Aleksandra, Igor Bukovsky, Emilie Rembert, Willy Yonas, Jihad Alwarith, Neal D. Barnard, and Hana Kahleova. "The Effects of Vegetarian and Vegan Diets on Gut Microbiota." *Frontiers in Nutrition* (April 17, 2019), frontiersin.org/articles/10.3389/fnut.2019.00047/full.

Tran, Elisabeth, Hanna Fjeldheim Dale, Caroline Jensen, and Gülen Arslan Lied. "Effects of Plant-Based Diets on Weight Status: A Systematic Review." *Diabetes, Metabolic Syndrome and Obesity: Targets and Therapy* (September 30, 2020), ncbi.nlm.nih.gov/pmc/articles/PMC7533223.

USA Pulses, "Get Cooking." usapulses.org/consumers/get-cooking.

Wang, Xia, Yingying Ouyang, Jun Liu, Minmin Zhu, Gang Zhao, Wei Bao, and Frank B Hu. "Fruit and Vegetable Consumption and Mortality From All Causes, Cardiovascular Disease, and Cancer: Systematic Review and Dose-Response Meta-Analysis of Prospective Cohort Studies." *British Medical Journal* (July 29, 2014), bmj.com/content/349/bmj.g4490.

Whole Grains Council, "Cooking Whole Grains." wholegrainscouncil.org/recipes/cooking-whole-grains.

Xu, Xiaoming, Prateek Sharma, Shijie Shu, Tzu-Shun Lin, Philippe Ciais, Francesco N. Tubiello, Pete Smith, Nelson Campbell, and Atul K. Jain. "Global Greenhouse Gas Emissions From Animal-Based Foods Are Twice Those of Plant-Based Foods." *Nature News* (September 13, 2021), nature.com/articles/s43016-021-00358-x.

INDEX

ABOUT THE AUTHOR

Marisa Moore is an award-winning registered dietitian nutritionist with a background in clinical nutrition, wellness, and the food industry. As a trusted expert in communication and nutrition, she encourages a practical and balanced approach to wellness focused on what you *can* eat, including plenty of fruit, vegetables, legumes, nuts, grains, healthy fats, and fish. Before launching her consultancy, Moore worked as an outpatient dietitian in diabetes education, was the corporate nutritionist in research and development for a national restaurant chain, and managed the employee worksite nutrition program at the U.S. Centers for Disease Control and Prevention (CDC). Her science-based nutrition advice and popular blog have made her a well-known expert, and she has been featured in *People* magazine, the *New York Times*, the *Wall Street Journal*, and on NBC Nightly News. She has made regular appearances on CNN and other networks. She is also a contributing editor for *Food & Nutrition Magazine*. She lives in Atlanta, Georgia. For more recipe ideas and plant-forward tips, follow her on Instagram and TikTok (@marisamoore), or visit her website, *marisamoore.com*.

Since 1888, the National Geographic Society has funded more than 14,000 research, conservation, education, and storytelling projects around the world. National Geographic Partners distributes a portion of the funds it receives from your purchase to National Geographic Society to support programs including the conservation of animals and their habitats.

Get closer to National Geographic Explorers and photographers, and connect with our global community. Join us today at nationalgeographic.org/joinus

For rights or permissions inquiries, please contact National Geographic Books Subsidiary Rights: bookrights@natgeo.com

All photographs by Marisa Moore except: front cover, Scott Suchman; 2-3, Svetl/Getty Images; 4, Scott Suchman; 6, Scott Suchman; 12, Mediterranean/Getty Images; 30, Scott Suchman; 38, IriGri8/Getty Images; 49, Donald Crossland/Getty Images; 65, Brett Stevens/Getty Images; 78, Scott Suchman; 96, Scott Suchman; 142, Scott Suchman; 186, Scott Suchman; 254, Scott Suchman.

Library of Congress Cataloging-in-Publication Data
Names: Moore, Marisa, author.
Title: The plant love kitchen : an easy guide to plant-forward eating, with 75+ recipes / Marisa Moore.
Description: [Washington] : National Geographic, [2023] | Includes index. | Summary: "Marisa Moore, R.D., offers a flexible approach to a more plant-forward diet that can improve your health"-- Provided by publisher.
Identifiers: LCCN 2022022402 (print) | LCCN 2022022403 (ebook) | ISBN 9781426222214 (hardcover) | ISBN 9781426223242 (ebook)
Subjects: LCSH: Vegetarian cooking. | Vegan cooking. | Cooking (Natural foods) | LCGFT: Cookbooks.
Classification: LCC TX837 .M6667 2023 (print) | LCC TX837 (ebook) | DDC 641.5/6362--dc23/eng/20220524
LC record available at https://lccn.loc.gov/2022022402
LC ebook record available at https://lccn.loc .gov/2022022403

ISBN: 978-1-4262-2221-4

Printed in China

22/RRDH/1